I have known Dave for more than 2 decades. He is a community planning professional and a people person. I introduced Dave to CESO in 2011 and I am delighted to have done that. This book sums up his experiences in the Philippines, Central and South America, Africa and Mongolia and some of his other travels. He has done some outstanding work where he helped communities facing dire economic and social challenges. You will be inspired by what he has done, his incites into sustainable planning and by the fascinating stories being told.

— **Jag Dhillon FCIP, Retired Planner**
  CESO Volunteer for over 30 years

Dave Smith is a fearless CESO Advisor. He is not afraid of getting out of his comfort zone in order to help CESO Clients, even in very remote places in the Philippines. and he does not complain if his accommodation is not comfortable. His assignments took place in island provinces and municipalities where he had to ride boats and be transported by motorcycle and walk kilometers, to do his work in the field. Our Clients (Local Government Units, Cooperatives and the Department of Trade and Industry) were comfortable working with him and singing karaoke together after the days' work. A very remarkable Canadian, truly a friend of Filipinos! We thank him for his help in improving the lives of our CESO Clients.

— **Matt Navalta**
  Philippine Country Representative, CESO

My brother, brave, sometimes "on the edge," busy with his life all over the world as a CESO volunteer. He has been places and has stories to tell about his journeys.... some funny, some involving risk and all interesting, written in a manner that will either have you smiling or "shaking your head."

— **Bob Smith**
  Brother

Dave has been my friend and a guest lecturer in the Geography Department for about 15 years. He comes prepared with information on the geographic, social and economic conditions from countries where he has worked and visited. Most of his presentations are from the many CESO projects he has undertaken and some "wow" stories from his traveling. Those lectures are always well received. Yes – I am now in my 60's and Dave demonstrates there is a lot of learning, fun and excitement to be had after 60.

— **Dr. Carlos Teixeira Ph.D**
  Geography Department
  University of British Columbia, Okanagan

Dave first came to Colombia in 2016. He worked on an assignment in Pijao and also as a lead advisor for partnership action plans within the coffee triangle of Colombia. While these assignments were a lot of work, they also entailed field trips to rural mountain areas where he was exposed to the true Colombian culture. He worked with people in advancing community development and fostering public engagement in the process. Everyone worked together well on his various trips here up until 2020. Dave is now an "amigo" to many Colombians.

— **Natalia Naranjo Ramos**
  Country Representative, CESO Colombia

After 60

and On the Edge
Like Indiana Jones

*Amazing Experiences Through
Volunteering and Travel*

David Thomas Smith

◆ FriesenPress

One Printers Way
Altona, MB R0G 0B0
Canada

www.friesenpress.com

ISBN
978-1-03-912103-4 (Hardcover)
978-1-03-912102-7 (Paperback)
978-1-03-912104-1 (eBook)

1. Biography & Autobiography, Business

Distributed to the trade by The Ingram Book Company

Eating a python snake (Sawa) in Lucban, Philippines in 2012)

Table of Contents

ix   **Introduction**

1   **Chapter 1: HONDURAS**
The Assignment in San Pedro Sula, Honduras and Exploring Parts of Honduras in 2011

14   **Chapter 2: LUCBAN IN THE PHILIPPINES**
Assignments in 2012 and 2014

29   **Chapter 3: THE PHILIPPINES**
Encounters with Typhoons and Tropical Storms

38   **Chapter 4: THE PHILIPPINES**
Assignments in Alabat Island and the Polillo Group of Islands Between 2013 and 2019

63   **Chapter 5: THE PHILIPPINES**
Assignments in the Northern Batanes Islands in 2017 and Bulacan State University in 2019

72   **Chapter 6: THE PHILIPPINES**
Exploring Parts of the Visayas Region and the Palawan Islands: 2012 – 2017

81   **Chapter 7: THE PHILIPPINES**
Exploring Areas in Northern Luzon: 2012-2017

91   **Chapter 8: THE PHILIPPINES**
Finding a Way to Help the Philippines While in Canada: Solar Electricity for Remote Schools in the Polillo Group of Islands

96   **Chapter 9: COLOMBIA**
The Coffee Triangle Assignments and Exploring Parts of Colombia: 2016-2019

121   **Chapter 10: ETHIOPIA**
Assignments in Bahir Dar and Addis Ababa and Exploring Parts of Ethiopia in 2019 and 2020

143   **Chapter 11: MONGOLIA**
The Mongolia Assignment and Exploring a Frontier Like No Other in 2017

157   **Chapter 12: CHINA**
Exploring Hong Kong and Beijing in 2012 and 2017

173   **Chapter 13: SURINAME AND JAMAICA**
Assignments in Two Countries of the Caribbean World and Explorations While There in : Suriname 2017 and Jamaica in 2019

192   **Chapter 14: CONCLUSION**
Nearly a Decade of Volunteering for CESO and the Adventures Travelling Abroad

195   **ACKNOWLEGEMENTS**

Introduction

We are born, and then go through life often not knowing or contemplating what comes next. That has certainly been true for me. This is a story about my life's experiences and adventures, emphasizing life after sixty, which I have to say, "turned my life on its head."

The book is entitled, *After Sixty and on the Edge like Indiana Jones: Amazing Experiences through Volunteering and Travel*. In looking back, the first sixty years of my life were structured, predictable and comfortable, although they involved some job displacements, a divorce, and the heartbreaking deaths of my mother and father. And so life goes. The Oxford dictionary definition of an Indiana Jones experience is "a person who regularly gets into exciting, dangerous, and sometimes humorous situations", and that was certainly not my life before sixty.

I began my life in the most conservative place on the planet—a small-town Mennonite community near Winnipeg, Manitoba, called Steinbach. This was a good place to grow up; a safe, friendly, small community on the Canadian prairies. I grew up with cold winters, short summers, mosquitoes, hailstorms, and often not a very hospitable climate, but as expressed by Nietzsche, "what doesn't kill you makes you stronger." I survived.

My family members were typical WASP (White Anglo-Saxon Protestants). Our parents were transplanted into the deeply religious, predominantly Mennonite community. My father was a banker, and before my brother and I were born, he was transferred from Winnipeg to Steinbach to be the branch manager for the Royal Bank of Canada in the community. Steinbach was an unusual place. It might have had the highest number of churches per capita in Canada. It was a dry town—no alcohol sales were permitted within the corporate limits of that town in those days (one of the few places like that in the country). In the 1960s, the school prohibited girls from wearing make-up or short skirts. Sunday was "the Lord's Day of rest," so almost no stores were open. I recall an incident where my friends and I were kicked off the community hockey rink on a Sunday just because it was Sunday. The city of Winnipeg was only a one-hour drive away, but it was much different there and those stricter religious-based rules did not apply.

My excitement growing up was sports and to this day, they have always been a big part of my life. My first exposure to inter-cultural exchanges was through playing hockey and baseball with the Mennonite kids, who often spoke a low German dialect. Our team played against opponents of French and Ukrainian descent. In that competitive environment, I learned words from these languages. I became well versed in foul language at a multi-cultural level. Unfortunately, I did not have more language proficiency aside from that.

I had a nice, safe, and happy childhood. My upbringing and the family household were very stable. My father was a bank manager, well respected, a community leader, and an inspiration. My mother stayed at home, and my brother and I were well taken care of by her. Both, of course, have passed, but they will forever be remembered and loved. As life unfolded, my brother and I were steered into university by our parents, and subsequently into great careers—my brother Bob, a lawyer for forty-five years and myself, a city planner for forty years.

So what was my life before sixty like? I was married twice, raised five children and one stepdaughter, and I now have two grandchildren. I am quite proud of that. Before sixty, I stayed close to home and life was usually quite predictable. In my working career, after obtaining my Master of City Planning degree from the University of Manitoba in 1977, I moved away from my home in Manitoba to Saskatchewan, where I worked for about one year in Regina. During that time, there was an ad posted for a city planner in Moose Jaw—a great challenge, the first city planner to be hired by that city. I was only twenty-six and a bit young for a job like that, but as time went on, I was quite successful. I stayed there for just over thirteen years. Following a restructuring in the city, several city positions were eliminated, including mine. I moved from Saskatchewan with wife and two young children in 1992, and went on to work in several local government positions in different cities:

- Port Alberni, British Columbia, city planner (1992-2000).
- Edmonton, Alberta (Strathcona County), planning coordinator (2000-2002)
- Fort St. John, BC, director of planning and engineering (2002-2005)
- Regional District surrounding Port Alberni, BC, director of planning (2005-2006)
- Sioux Lookout, Ontario, manager of development services (2006)
- District of Peachland, BC, director of planning and development services (2007-2013)
- Smithplan Consulting, private consultant (2014-2019).

These years in my public sector and private consulting career were certainly not of the "Indiana Jones" variety. I am not sure why that was the case and why I resisted a more adventurous path. Perhaps it was because of scary world events taking place over time that shaped my thinking. I can recall the Cold War (until 1989), the assassination of President Kennedy (1964), the eruption of Mount St. Helens (1980), the Chernobyl nuclear disaster (1986), the 9-11 twin towers terrorist attacks (2001) and the wildfires taking place near my West Kelowna home and the rushed evacuation of my family (2009)—these were fearful events shaping my thinking and perhaps they dampened my desire for world travel in my years before sixty. But things did change!

I had a friend and work colleague named Jag Dhillon, a fellow planner and an Indo-Canadian, who was a member of a non-profit economic development organization called CESO (the Canadian Executive Service Organization). CESO is dedicated to promoting economic development and empowerment by growing sustainable, inclusive businesses and strengthening businesses. Jag did some work for me as a consultant while I was the director of planning in Peachland, BC. In discussions with Jag, he informed me about CESO. Jag had undertaken over thirty projects on behalf of CESO, and he encouraged me to try this. At first, I thought "no way". But after thinking about it – maybe this would be a good thing to do in retirement, even though I had never envisioned doing it. I decided to go through the application process and do the advance training. I was eventually enrolled as a CESO advisor. Strangely enough, the CESO enrollment coincided with May 2011, the time I turned sixty.

I began travelling and doing assignments for CESO, and it transformed me. It became a major focus for my life and a good way to make a valuable contribution and transition into retirement. I travelled to many places and enjoyed every assignment I completed. So much so, that I volunteered to go to quite remote places, within the countries which I visited. Those countries are shown on the map following this chapter. Matt Navalta, the CESO Country Representative in the Philippines, casually referred to me as the "Indiana Jones of CESO." Through subsequent assignments there, the label seemed to stick.

I need to say a few words about CESO. This organization changed my life. Working and collaborating with partners, CESO helps deliver sustainable development results in response to local needs. They assemble skilled and experienced Canadians with expertise to work with developing countries in meeting their goals. I was very lucky to be one of them. Some assignment outcomes are more successful than others, but all of them, from what I could see, add value to the sponsoring group within that country. CESO takes care of all of their volunteer advisors wherever they go.

My favourite TV show that I used watch was *Parts Unknown* featuring the late Anthony Bourdain. This show was about the adventures of a travelling chef, including some of his deep-thinking worldly analysis. This program played a role in changing my mindset from being a stay-at-home person to becoming a world traveler. Indeed, I tell stories in this book in a comparable way to how Anthony Bourdain did on *Parts Unknown*. You will notice this book is a combination of my travel and CESO work experience mixed with a bit of geo-political commentary.

At the time of writing this book, I had been a member of CESO for nine years, and completing twenty-three international assignments in seven developing countries in Asia, South America, and Africa. It has been an amazing experience filled with adventure, rewarding work, and new friendships. What a wonderful world life can offer us, even after sixty!

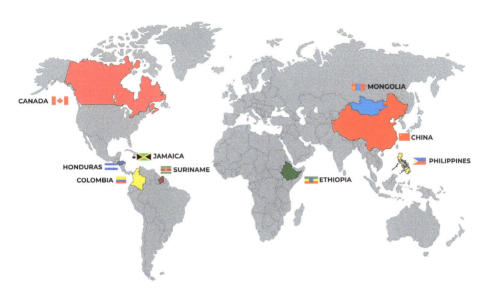

Map showing the countries in the world which I visited since 2011
Map prepared by Lance Smith

Chapter 1

....

HONDURAS

*The Assignment in San Pedro Sula, Honduras
and Exploring Parts of Honduras in 2011*

Map prepared by Lance Smith

About Honduras

Honduras is the second largest and second most populous country in Central America. The population in 2011 was 8,481,000. [1] Its land area is about 112,100 square kilometers compared to the province of British Columbia (BC), Canada with an area of 944,700 square kilometers. [2,3] Honduras's land mass is only 11.9 percent as large as BC, but it is about three times larger than Vancouver Island. The country is bordered by Guatemala to the northwest, El Salvador to the south, and Nicaragua to the southeast. It has colonial villages, natural parks, and a Pacific and Caribbean coastline with the Bay Islands that contains great beaches and coral reefs, where tourists go for exceptional snorkeling and diving. In my two weeks in Honduras, I did not see these, but I did see ancient Mayan ruins (Copan), some wild areas, fruit plantations (bananas and pineapple), magnificent wood carvings and other souvenirs, delicious cuisine, and everyday city life.

My time in Honduras in 2011 was less than two years after a major over-throw in government, whereby leftist leader Manuel Zalaya caused a constitutional crisis because of his attempt to rewrite the Honduras constitution. He was thrown out of office by the army after only 2 years in power in power and he was deported to Costa Rica. This was an intense time. [4]

Political instability has been a big part of Honduras history. Apart from Indigenous populations, the Spanish have had a very dominant influence on the culture, from the Spanish entry (Christopher Columbus) in the 1500s and occupation up until 1821. The population mix was also influenced by a significant migration from Germany after World War II. About 3 percent of the population is of Lebanese descent, and they have been a substantial presence in the business community. Foreign influences from multi-national corporations and from the US government have also been significant.

Travelling to San Pedro Sula

Honduras was my first international assignment. In looking back, I was so naïve. The notion of travelling to a distant, foreign place with a unique language, culture, and climate was a huge change to the pattern of my life. I was both excited and nervous. It was a lengthy plane ride—Kelowna to Seattle, and then to Houston (Alaska Air); Houston to San Pedro Sula (Continental Airways). I arrived at the San Pedro Sula airport on August 22, 2011—it was not only hot, but ghastly hot. The shuttle service was provided by the sponsoring client and Samantha Sabbion, CANTURH Executive Director, picked me up on time. CANTURH was the tourism agency for San Pedro Sula. I checked into the comfortable Hotel Las Cascades, near the downtown and that went well.

The CESO Assignment—
The Creation of Tourist Zones in San Pedro Sula

Before coming to my first CESO assignment in San Pedro Sula, I put a lot of effort into being well prepared and orchestrating a serious two-week schedule to create a plan and program for establishing tourist zones in the city. I had requested a program including research, investigation, and consultation among stakeholders. I asked CANTURH—the privately run tourism sponsoring organization—to set up workshops and include many stakeholders. These invited representatives were to include businesses, local government, departmento (provincial) government agencies, politicians, the media, and universities. In San Pedro Sula, it became somewhat apparent that CANTURH, and many of the people in Honduras, were reluctant to engage with government. In Honduras, government participation and engagement was not the way things were normally done. Governments made the rules, the people and organizations followed them. My experience as a planner and public servant in Canada was that things get done through collabouration and consensus, usually involving government. The host client eventually agreed and set-up a workshop, which was well attended by invited stakeholder groups and several government officials.

The meeting was interesting! At first, the dignitaries spoke, then I gave a presentation in English, translated into Spanish by the CESO country representative for Honduras, Graciela Galeano Burgos, and she did a great job. The audience were quiet at first, but suddenly, the participants began to ask questions and make comments:

"Where will the money come from?" "How will different agencies work together?" "The streets are unlit and dangerous at night—will there be better lighting and better security?" "Overhead utility cables and power lines are a mess—can non-working lines be removed?" "Can the city do a better job of removing litter on the streets?" "Can the heavy traffic be improved?"

It was nice to see many government agencies and politicians represented. Problems were shared, answers to questions raised in discussions were provided, and new approaches were suggested to improve the city image and governance issues. Despite some initial hesitation in participating, I have to say that meeting was impressive, respectful, and productive.

One thing I almost screwed up. I had prepared a lengthy PowerPoint presentation and after having taken an introductory Spanish course in Canada, I thought I knew some Spanish words. I took it upon myself to try to encapsulate the workshop presentation slide headings in Spanish. About ten minutes before the presentations began, Henning Kretchmer, the CANTURH president, checked over my slides and he just about had a heart attack. He scrambled to correct those titles and saved me a lot of embarrassment. Lesson learned—my Spanish was still unacceptable.

As for the formal assignment undertaken, I have to say it went quite well. There were tours and investigations within and nearby San Pedro Sula, as well as workshop sessions. The two workshops were well-attended. Valuable input was received and recommendations for six tourist zones within the city were incorporated into the final workshop presentation. The final report was completed for the client and CESO in Canada. The media attended both sessions, and the event was reported in the city's largest newspapers and my picture hit the press with quotes—all in Spanish. For a brief period, I was famous in San Pedro Sula, Honduras.

Media Coverage – My Picture in City Newspapers

The workshop presentations were held in an exclusive business club complex. I think this place was for rich and highly successful businesspeople in San Pedro Sula. Called the Honduran Arab Social Center, it was surrounded by high walls with barbed wire on top. The entrances to the complex were guarded by soldier-like security guards, all well-armed. In order to enter this complex, papers or identification was required. It was intimidating for me being a Canadian who was not used to such things. While the sessions were very good, the transparent and open process got somewhat hampered by those intimidating circumstances. But at least the media coverage was provided. I did not expect to have my picture and this CESO project highlighted in Honduran newspapers, so that was a pleasant surprise.

San Pedro Sula—High Crime Rate and Lack of Gun Control

Honduras has one of the world's highest murder rates, due mostly to rampant gangs —mostly in San Pedro Sula, where I happened to be located for most of my two-week stay. There is apparently a very flawed firearm regulatory system in place. In Honduras, most people bypass the country's gun registration system and obtain firearms on the black market. [5]

On my shuttle trips throughout San Pedro Sula, I was shocked—I did not understand why the city looked so different than anywhere else I had ever been. Walls, fences, and barbed wire surrounded every property. My first thoughts were: I am an urban planner, and aesthetics are important. A friendly atmosphere and positive image are essential. Good architecture is something that should not be hidden. There were soldiers in military gear everywhere. Security guards in front of every commercial property, equipped with guns, often machine guns. At financial institutions and banks, I often saw guards and their guns protecting these buildings. At the entry into government buildings, banks, major stores, or shopping malls, guards did body frisking for security before entering those facilities.

At first, I was afraid of those guards and soldiers. After a few days, I got used to seeing them everywhere, and even had my picture taken with them. Hondurans told me, the guards are there to protect the people, don't be afraid of them.

I recall after the long flight to Honduras, I went to the hotel and rested. As it got dark, I heard strange noises outside from the streets. It sounded like the constant popping of popcorn. I asked the people at the hotel what the noise was. They said—oh it's likely just people shooting their guns in the air. It was suggested I not go out at night, and I didn't, but these warnings were still worrisome.

A Dangerous Person Near the Hotel

The guard at the hotel told me that it was safe to walk around during the daytime in the area surrounding the hotel, so I did wander out during the day on a few occasions. Although that advice was mostly true, I did experience a terrifying encounter. On one occasion, I walked down the street and crossed to the mid-boulevard, which was well landscaped with shaded trees. It was mostly obstructed from the vision of the passing traffic. As I reached the boulevard, a desperate man with a large machete dangling from his belt approached me. His hands were out toward me, and he was demanding that I give him money. He did not know any English, and he kept flexing his arms, requesting *lampira*, the Honduran currency. Then it looked like he was going to pull out his machete, but instead he ripped open the entire front side of his T-shirt and exposed the biggest scar I had ever seen, extending from his throat to his belt buckle. His demands became louder and his gestures scarier and threatening. Reacting quickly, I kept saying "no entiendo Espanol." This back-and-forth exchange went on a few times, but it seemed like a lifetime. I eventually saw a gap in the traffic. I ran as fast as I could, across the boulevard and down the street, about three blocks back to the hotel. I did not see that guy chasing me back to the hotel, but I was not looking behind to find out. That is an incident I will never forget.

An Encounter with a Street Seller

I saw a lot of poverty in Honduras. There were those who have jobs and money and those who struggle. Like other developing countries I visited over the years, in Honduras there were many street beggars who ask you for money. While my instinct was to try to help, often people nearby are watching you. If you remove your wallet in crowded quarters, you can easily get robbed. I recall being driven back to the hotel one day by Samantha Sabbion. The air-conditioning in her car did not work, and the car windows needed to be open or we would have cooked. We approached a traffic circle, slowed down, and eventually stopped due to the merging traffic. There were street sellers who used this as a strategic selling point. One of the sellers approached the car, leaned head-first through the window, and tried to place sunglasses on my face. I did not want those sunglasses, but he persisted in his aggressive selling. I was able to hand the glasses back to the seller and close the car window, but it was not an easy thing to do. Wow, that was another unforgettable adventure!

Visiting the Mayan Ruins

Because I had seen those iconic Indiana Jones movies about the adventures of this renowned professor of archeology, I thought seeing ruins would be a "must do" experience. As part of my CESO assignment in Honduras, I was able to see three ruin sites. I saw the UNESCO world renowned Mayan ruin site at Copan, which I visited on the weekend when I did not work on the assignment. This was a very popular tourist destination. However, en-route from San Pedro Sula to Copan, there were five checkpoints where guards stopped all vehicles and checked ID's or passports, and it was always somewhat unsettling when this happened. I also visited two more recently discovered Mayan ruins, the Curruste site and the Rancho El Ocotillo site, located near San Pedro Sula, both having had very little site reclamation done. These two ruins were not established tourist destinations at that point.

The Copan Ruins were an amazing tourist attraction of impactful historic significance. I had a tour guide take me through the site, and she provided interesting background historical information. She told me the ruins were constructed as far back as 300 AD and were abandoned by the Mayan culture just before 900 AD. The site consisted of pyramid structures including temples, plazas, alter complexes, and ball courts. I was informed that the Maya site of Copan represents one of the spectacular achievements of the classic Mayan period because of the number and magnitude of its architectural and sculptural monuments. I was taken through tunnels underground and shown alter structures where humans and animals were sacrificed to the gods, and their blood drank as part of the ritual. That was eerie . . . I certainly had not known about these things.

Other Lesser Known Ruins in Honduras

The Curruste and Rancho El Coco burial sites are located just outside of San Pedro Sula. The mounds have been discovered in the past few decades, but sufficient funds are not available in Honduras to conduct excavation digs, so the mounds remain mostly undisturbed. These ruins are still mostly underneath the sediment and vegetation. The officials asked me to make enquiries to universities in Canada to see if there would be any interest. I made enquiries, but I did not have success in this regard. Not many people outside of Honduras know about these sites. I feel fortunate to have seen these places. Perhaps there is excavation is taking place now.

The host also gave me a tour of the Museo de Antropologia e Historia (Museum of Anthropology and History) and the Galaria National de Arte San Pedro Sula (National Art Gallery of San Pedro Sula). These were very impressive facilities with quality displays and full of educational information. The Museum of Anthropology and History was extremely professionally done and with detailed articulate displays. The art gallery also showcased the works of many impressive artists within San Pedro Sula and throughout Honduras. I met the curator, a Honduran educated in Montreal.

Amazing Souvenirs of Honduras

I need to mention a pleasant surprise I experienced—the high quality, beautiful souvenirs I discovered in markets in San Pedro Sula—amazing, especially the wood carving and the leather goods such as boots, shoes, jackets, and purses and bags. I brought back some nice souvenirs, including a pair of cowboy boots and an embroidered leather belt. There are two excellent places to shop in Honduras. One is the central plaza, with a large number of souvenir shops and restaurants. The central plaza was attractive, surrounded by the Cathedral de San Pedro Apóstol, the city's largest Catholic church, and City Hall. The other souvenir place is the Quamilito Market, a short taxi ride from the downtown. This is a huge market structure, the size of a couple of hockey arenas in Canada, and it is full of interesting things to see and purchase. I suggest that anyone travelling to Honduras do souvenir shopping.

Visiting the Downtown Plaza Area

During my visit downtown with CANTURH officials, there were people demonstrating and carrying signs. Not all in that city were happy with the departure of the former president. I was told to be careful while in this area because as a foreigner, I would be considered by as a "gringo." I could be an easy target for a thief, or I could be mistaken as American, and many Hondurans do not see Americans in a favourable light. My hosts suggested I should never go downtown without local accompaniment, so I only got to see that area on one occasion, but it was impressive.

The Dole Banana Plantation

My hosts took me on a tour of the Dole banana plantation about one hour outside of San Pedro Sula. The Dole Company is an American agricultural multi-national corporation headquartered in California. They told me during the tour that the company is the largest producer of fruit and vegetables in the world. I saw the entire banana agricultural production process taking place through to the shipping process. For me this was an interesting experience, and I enjoyed this trip very much. It was fascinating to see how the bananas in the trees were wrapped in plastic. When ripe, they were picked, washed, graded, cut in stems with eight bananas, and then put into boxes. There was careful quality control. A lot of fruit got rejected. The boxes were loaded and shipped out in trucks at the site.

Possible Parkland Areas or Ecological Protection Areas

A couple of other sites near San Pedro Sula were explored for potential tourist destinations. There was the Jucutuma Lagoon, a former lake area experiencing ecological change that contained a wide variety of plant, wildlife, bird, and marine species, but evasive aquatic plant species were dominating the area. It would take a lot of work to restore the lagoon back to its natural condition, but it had a lot of potential for development as a park, with both a natural area and space for more active recreation such as camping, hiking, or possibly a centre for a business retreat. They also showed me a jungle area containing an abundance of tropical plants, which they referred to as the El Ocotillo Botanical Park. The area was being used as a nursery to grow and transplant attractive vegetation throughout the city. It was, however, located adjacent to the municipal landfill site, so there were some impediments in turning it into a botanical park tourist attraction.

Soccer—The National Sport of Honduras

I love sports, and a few days before my departure, there was an evening World Cup qualifying football (soccer) game taking place between Honduras and I believe Costa Rica. I had asked to go to the game, but the hosts did not want me to go there. I guess the football fans were quite wild and there was frequently a lot of reckless behavior and fighting in the stands, and the hosts were not comfortable taking me there and they wanted me to be safe. The closest I got to the game was when we drove past that stadium.

The Return Home from Honduras

I left San Pedro Sula in September 2011, and I was hoping for an uneventful trip back home to Canada. Not quite! Although the Continental Airlines flight left on time, we encountered a severe tropical storm approaching the Houston airport. The turbulence was perhaps the worst I have ever experienced in an airplane. As we approached the runway, the wings of that Boeing 777 began to rock side to side and seemed to be out of control. I was watching and we were just about to touch down, but the rocking was so severe the pilot increased the thrust and took off again before landing, over-shooting the runway. The turbulence was unbelievable. We reached higher altitude, things improved a bit, and I think we circled the Houston airport three or four times, resulting in an hour delay. We were finally able to land. Upon landing, there was a loud cheer from all the passengers, rivaling crowd noise from any hockey game I have ever attended in Canada. Hurray . . . I survived!

A Disruptive Scene on the Airplane

I was barely able to make the flight connection from Houston to Seattle on Continental Airlines. There was just one more flight that day on Alaska Airways, from Seattle to Kelowna. I thought this flight would be routine, but not so. Upon getting seated on the aircraft, something seemed wrong. There was a lady who got on the plane who did not have a ticket. She was noisy, aggressive, and refused to leave the airplane. The crew tried unsuccessfully to have her leave the aircraft, but she would not comply. The staff left and came back several times, trying to convince the lady to leave. She would not. Finally, some armed security personnel came onto the plane and forcefully removed her, kicking and screaming, past my seat, through the aircraft, and out of the airplane. After that, the plane left, and I returned safely to Canada and to my home. At least that crazy lady was not a terrorist.

Honduras in the Rear View Mirrow

Life in Honduras was a lot different than in Canada. This trip was an "eye-opener" for me—especially for someone who was not so well travelled. But Honduras was a beautiful country with friendly, hospitable people. Safety and security, poverty, jobs—these were, and still are, such big issues in Honduras—especially in San Pedro Sula. We complain a lot about things in Canada. I kept thinking after that trip that we really do not have so much to complain about, considering our stable economy, social safety net, greater restrictions on firearms, and our healthcare system. The people of Honduras desire a safer and better future. I hope they can find a way to overcome the obstacles in their way. There is potential for that country. It has many assets, but the struggles seem to continue.

FOOTNOTES

1. The Worldbank Data as cited in Wikipedia
2. CIA World Factbook and other sources (2011) as cited in Wikipedia
3. The Geography of British Columbia, Canada; J. Lewis Robinson (updated May 20, 2020) as cited in Wikipedia
4. Mica Rosenburg, Honduran Troops Surround Presidential Palace, Reuters News (June 28, 2009) article cited in Wikipedia
5. Dudley, Steven, **Counting Firearms in Honduras,** Insight Crime (August 23, 2017); as cited in Wikipedia

Pictures of San Pedro Sula and Places in Honduras in 2011

From top left: CESO session panel; Assignment Work Group; Public engagement; Newspaper coverage; Security walls in San Pedro Sula; Area of mugging attempt; Guarded residential area; Street sellers in traffic; Copan ruins; Copan ruins; Curriste burial site; Rancho El Coco burial site

Pictures of San Pedro Sula and Places in Honduras in 2011

From top left: Museo de Antropologica e Historia; Honduras souvenirs; Dole banana plantation; Dole banana plant; Dole banana shipping; San Pedro Sula central plaza; Jucutuma Lagoon; El Octillo Nursery – Botanical Garden; Soccer stadium in San Pedro Sula; Local street; Rural area housing

Chapter 2

....

LUCBAN IN THE PHILIPPINES

Assignments in 2012 and 2014

Map prepared by Lance Smith

An Overview of the Philippines

The Philippines contains a population of about 100 million people, with an estimated 10 million additional citizens working abroad. Metro Manila is one of the largest cities in the world with about 20 million people. [1] The total land area of the Philippines is around 300,000 square kilometers, with an overall population density of 360 per square kilometers. In comparing that to the province of British Columbia in Canada, our population is about 4.6 million on a land area of 944,700 square kilometers—more than three times larger than the land mass of the Philippines and with a population density of only 4.8 people per kilometer. [2] It becomes obvious for anyone travelling to the Philippines is that there are a lot of people living in this small country.

The Philippines faces formidable challenges. From my observations, I saw a significant amount of poverty, high population growth, under-employment, persistent and systemic levels of corruption (especially at higher levels of government), inadequate infrastructure, and an underperforming agricultural system. Major environmental disasters also occur that affect the country from time to time, such as tropical storms, typhoons, and earthquakes. I was informed of a high rate of crime and terrorism in the Mindinao area of the southern Philippines as well, although I never travelled to that part of the country. But my trips to the Philippines were both enjoyable and adventurous.

In working in the Philippines, and later in other places in that country, I developed a good relationship with Matt Navalta, the CESO Country Representative (CR). Matt was perhaps the most organized CR of any of the countries where I worked. He is also an excellent karaoke singer and musician, and he has become a good friend. I believe this connection and the success of my earlier assignments in this country, helped me to get recruited for other assignments there.

Visiting Lucban in 2012 and 2014

The town of Lucban has a population of about 50,000, and it lies about a three-and-a half-hour drive south of Manila on the main island of Luzon. [3] I arrived in Lucban in late November 2012. I had been selected by CESO-SACO to complete a project for a master tourism plan for the town, and it was a thrill for me to be selected to go there and do that.

My wife, who is a Canadian of Filipino descent, was excited for me and our four children (Riley, Dylan, Danika, and stepdaughter Nicole) to go to her country for the first time. They joined me after the first ten days of the CESO assignment in Lucban, and we enjoyed an extended vacation. As for me, I had inside information about the local culture and some knowledge of the Tagalog, the national language of the Philippines. I was prepared, as this was the homeland of my wife.

Pick-up at Manila Airport

A significant lesson on Filipino culture was learned quite quickly. My plane arrived at the Manila airport at four-thirty in the morning, and I recall how hot it was, and when exiting the plane, how the heat and humidity were overwhelming, even at 5am. It took about an hour to go through customs and retrieve my baggage from the carousel. I was to be picked up at the airport by the host—LGU Lucban—and I was supposed to look for an individual holding up a sign with my name on it. I went to the pick-up area and there was nobody there for me. I felt a sense of panic, so I phoned long distance to the CESO office in Toronto. I was able to speak to the project coordinator, Mai Nyguyen. After another hour of waiting, my ride eventually arrived. I was subsequently told this is "Filipino time," being late is the norm and patience is a virtue. This can often be a source of frustration for foreigners.

But I have to say, the level of hospitality and the degree of respect shown by Lucban officials and other Filipinos, was exceptional. They demonstrated greater respect and better manners than I had ever experienced in my own country, or anywhere else. I was often addressed as "sir," and they referred to me as an "expert." I was in professional planning practice in Canada for about four decades, and I seldom recall being addressed like that, so it was flattering and a definite compliment from wonderful people. I think they know, "flattery will get you anywhere."

Travelling to Lucban

It was a long, difficult journey. It was a fourteen-hour flight, including waiting time at airports and a four-hour drive from Manila to Lucban by Philippine Airlines. I got almost no sleep. I was introduced to the mayor and the vice mayor on arrival in Lucban. I felt quite uncomfortable because I was so tired, feeling grubby, and in need of a shower, but the meeting with the mayor and staff went ok. My hotel, the Patio Rizal, was across the street from the municipal office where I was to work, and it faced the town's attractive central plaza, which was the main gathering place for people in the town. There were vendor kiosks and street food carts, and it was an active place for most of the day and night, much noisier than in my neighbourhood at home—but an interesting, happy place.

The CESO Assignment–A Tourism Action Plan for Lucban

The client, the local government unit (LGU) of Lucban, requested a tourism action plan for the community. My training in city planning was helpful in this regard. A planning process was followed and it involved compiling background information, field inspections, public engagement sessions with stakeholders, and completion of a final report with recommendations. The university in Lucban sent the tourism class to all public engagement sessions, and some students accompanied LGU officials and me on field inspections as well. A component of the assignment was to train LGU staff and students on the planning process and implementation of the plan. Lucban was not a coastal community with beaches, but there were still things of interest in the area. The plan highlighted a framework for their potential tourism and ways to attract visitors. It was well received, and it appeared to be a successful project.

Information about the Lucban area was obtained from the field trips taken within the town and surrounding areas. The information gathered was not only useful for the Lucban assignment, but also helpful for other CESO assignments done later in that country.

Work Protocol–The Monday Morning Ceremony

My exposure to the workplace in Lucban offered further interesting contrasts from Canadian perspectives. Every Monday morning, there was a ceremony where the mayor and top civic officials informed the municipal workers of the need for a strong commitment, ethics, and "God's influence" in public service required by the community. Prayers, the national anthem, and flag protocols took place. I was summoned to attend and without warning, and I was asked to address the large crowd of workers. I awkwardly offered greetings from Canada, and they seemed to be well received. This was a serious event. If a municipal worker did not attend, maybe there would be consequences? I believed there would be, judging from the tone of the messages communicated.

Although this ceremony was important to the work culture, it seemed to be a contrast to the overall public perception of government. Most citizens did not seem to have respect for the workings of government in general, especially at the higher levels. Governance in the Philippines was perceived as being corrupt and uncaring.

Filipinos Managing Resources Sustainably

We like to think of the Canadian, North American life being at a higher standard and superior to that of life in the Philippines or in other developing countries. I think that is an overly simplistic outlook. Canadians have a lot to learn. In my CESO work assignment, I had the opportunity to be taken on a tour of the local landfill site. What I experienced in that inspection was quite remarkable. I expected to see a lot of garbage and a disgusting pile of rubble. Instead, there was sorting, a large amount of composting, grinding of organic materials such as coconut shells and food and agricultural wastes, and further down the chain, soil bagging and product distribution. Also, rubber tires and various plastics were being repurposed and converted into bricks to be used for civic plazas and sidewalks. This was a particular initiative of Lito Nombrefia, the planning and engineering coordinator in Lucban at the town. I worked alongside Lito while I was there, and he also became a good friend. The efforts of this man, and the town, should be applauded. In my view, this was a rigorous, authentic, and cost-efficient effort in undertaking environmental recycling and re-use of waste–undertaken effectively, but with quite simple equipment by our standards.

Organic Farming

I saw impressive examples of organic farming taking place. Organic farming is labour intensive, and it is hard work. It produces healthier food. There are no chemicals used in the farming process. Three examples of organic farms were visited during this assignment—OISCA (in the Lucban region), the Costales Farm in Laguana (the province next to Lucban, Quezon) and the GK Farm in Bulacan (a province north of Manila)—and these were world class ventures.

In the Philippines, these enterprises were not simply technical solutions guided by legislation and overseen by the bureaucracy. They were passion-driven, mission-oriented projects. They were run by faith-based organizations or social enterprises and the mission was to grow healthier food for the population and alleviate the considerable poverty existing in the Philippines. At these farms, there were cottages on the lands used by college or university students in agricultural programs. There were units rented out to eco-tourists who want to experience an organic lifestyle. Other housing units were available for unemployed, low-income families, being trained as farm workers. The three enterprises were committed to the organic farming movement. They believed this was a global path to food security and it would be the way agriculture would be done in the future. I was extremely impressed.

A CESO Assignment Field Tour Ending and an Evening with Friends

There was another incredible evening, which I will never forget. It happened on a day when Lito took me on a tour, and we visited various facilities in the Lucban area. We saw the harvesting of coconuts in the jungle, processing plants for noodles, rice and *longanessa* sausage, as well as farms growing pineapples. After finishing the tour, Lito had arranged a dinner at his neighbourhood and there was a full meal provided—*pansit* (like chow mein) *lumpia* (like spring rolls) spicy chicken *adobo*, fish, and vegetables—lots of food. We drank Lambanog, a very potent home-distilled alcoholic drink, and there was beer and brandy available as well. We sang karaoke, and it was an amazing evening—at least from what I remember. Another Canadian who was also working on another CESO assignment in Lucban, Benoit Bouchard from Quebec, also joined us as a guest. Benoit was doing his assignment mostly indoors training the staff on electronic record keeping. He was happy to get out of the office to join us. He and I and our hosts were feeling pretty good as the evening continued. Maybe feeling too good!

To cap off the evening, some other neighbours from across the street had just cooked something that looked like a sushi roll, but not exactly. They said to me, "Sir, come and try this food." I replied, "Maybe I will, but tell me what it is first." They said, "Sir, you try it, and then we will tell you what it is." After going back and forth like that a few times, I finally agreed to try some. I did, and everyone laughed. They said, "Sir you just ate *sawa*—that is a python snake." I just about fell off the chair! It tasted quite different than anything else, but it had more bones in it than any fish I had ever had. It was a great evening, but I am curious—did Anthony Bourdain or Indiana Jones ever taste *sawa*?

Getting Around Filipino-style

Life in the Philippines is unique, particularly compared to North America. My first impressions had a powerful impact on me. Many of the vehicles they drove (called *tricycles* and *Jepnays*) were noticeably different forms of transportation than Canadians are used to. The Jepnays are like a Jeep with an extended cab. Tricycles are a motorcycle with a sidecar. These serve as transportation and the fares are more reasonable than taxis. Many smaller, low powered motorcycles (100-150cc motors) were also prevalent.

Stairway to Heaven—Kamay Ni Hesus

One of my favourite songs is "Stairway to Heaven" by Led Zeppelin. Well—I found where the stairway is. Kamay Ni Hesus in Lucban is a five-hectare religious shrine famous for its 300 steps, which climb to a statue of Jesus. This is a serious retreat—religious tourism, for prayer and healing. There are people who come here and say a prayer on every step—that would be a long day. I was informed that 90 percent of all people in the Philippines are of the Roman Catholic faith, and certainly there are prominent cathedrals/churches throughout the country. The Filipinos are profoundly serious about their faith. They believe things happen because it is "God's will." They have very deeply held beliefs and strong convictions.

Statues of Filipino Heroes

Heroes are worshipped in the Philippines. Statues and markers are everywhere paying tribute to historical events or their heroes such as Bonafasio, Rizal, Lapu Lapu and others. This way of displaying the nation's history was very interesting, and it made passersby take notice.

The 2012 Manny Pacquiao Fight

Speaking of a Filipino hero, Manny Pacquiao is a world champion boxer from the Philippines, and he is loved and cherished by everyone in that country. On December 8, 2012 there was a fight between Pacquiao and Juan Manuel Marquez from Mexico, which was shown on a giant screen at the municipal hall in Lucban. I was invited to attend, and I did. It was a noisy and emotional event for all watching, as everyone was pulling for Manny to win. It was a "full house", and I was the only Caucasian among hundreds in that hall. I felt a little awkward at first, but everyone was extremely friendly. As long as I cheered for Manny, I was "one of them." Unfortunately, Manny lost the fight, being knocked out, and everyone left the event feeling sad and disappointed.

Opening the Basketball Season and the Beauty Pageant

There was another major event happening in Lucban in early December, the opening of the basketball season. The vice mayor invited me to attend the event. It included all teams with their players in a marching parade, a rock-and-roll band at the court during the pre-game ceremony, and a beauty contest. I am sure the entire town showed up to watch. The citizens were extremely vocal and were having a blast that evening.

As I arrived at the basketball game, I was asked to sit in the VIP box with the mayor, vice mayor, and other dignitaries. They asked me to judge the beauty contest, and this took me by complete surprise. The girls were all beautiful, and how could I ever choose one over the others? I was out of my comfort zone on this one. I told them it was a tie, and they were all winners, but I think they wanted a better decision, so I probably failed in my duty.

A Christmas Party Like No Other

I have never seen people who like to celebrate Christmas more than Filipinos. In Lucban and throughout the Philippines, there are decorations on buildings and houses, and often with a strong religious theme. My wife and family joined me at a 1970s themed Christmas party celebration for Lucban town workers. This was the funniest event I have ever attended. All town workers wore attire of that era, music was playing, and as part of the program, the workers all marched like models on a runway, showing their outfits—prizes were given for the best. The emcee—a gay male, or "bakla", as they are called in the Philippines—dressed as a female and was tremendously entertaining. This was the most animated, funny performance for an emcee I have ever seen. Every sentence was a joke, mostly in the Tagaloc language, but it did not matter. There was total open-ness and absolutely no shame or shyness for this person being gay. I can only remember that after that evening, my stomach was sore for days from having laughed so much. . . punch line after punch line, almost never-ending—like Robin Williams and Adam Sandler on steroids.

The 2014 CESO Assignment at SLSU in Lucban—Adding Climate Change Courses to the University Programs

In May of 2014, I did a second CESO assignment in Lucban, Philippines at Southern Luzon State University (SLSU). This assignment was to assist the university faculties in developing climate change courses. It was a real pleasure to return to Lucban again. I was familiar with the town and the city staff, so I was able to forge a connection between the town and the university and this helped me to produce what turned out to be a high-quality report for them. A big problem in many areas of the Philippines was that there was no partnership between agencies – nobody talked to each other, and things did not get done properly. In this assignment, I tried to expose the stakeholders to a Canadian style of collabouration. It seemed to work.

PNEE—Philippine National Educators for the Environment

I was asked to be a speaker at the annual conference put on by the PNEE on the topic of climate challenge and sustainable planning. When I arrived at the event, I thought, "this is a really big deal—should I be here?" There were hundreds of academics from universities all over the Philippines and some from other countries. I was asked to speak at one of the PNEE seminars and to sit as part of a panel discussion. I was very nervous, as I did not usually present at such high-profile venues, although I did occasionally do guest lectures at UBCO (University of British Columbia) in Canada. But I was well prepared, and I had a pretty good background on the subject. As a director of planning in Peachland, BC, our community had received recognition as a BC Climate Action Community in 2012. That was because the Canadian municipality where I had worked had undertaken many measures to address climate change and sustainable planning. My presentation appeared to go well, and I learned a lot from my participation at that conference.

After the conference, the rest of the CESO assignment was devoted to working with the university and the faculty, developing university programs on climate change. The intention was to develop new courses and include them into their curriculums. I believe many of the assignment recommendations were implemented.

The San Isidro Pahiyas Festival in 2014

I happened to be doing the SLSU assignment in Lucban the same time that the famous annual San Isidro Pahiyas Festival was being held. What an amazing festival that was, I have never seen anything else like it—three days of events, a parade, music, dancing, games, merchandise being sold everywhere on the streets and plaza, and very large crowds. Every house in the town was decorated to the extreme. Due to this popular event, I was told there were no accommodations to be had anywhere near Lucban during the festival.

Filipino Cultural Dancing

During the assignment at the university, there was a fabulous social evening in which there was a Filipino cultural dancing taking place. The costumes and the dancing style are totally different than anything seen in North America. Candle dancing, bamboo dancing, and Spanish formal dancing—it was truly amazing and it was very enjoyable watching these very talented dancers.

A Funeral Procession in the Philippines

During my assignment in Lucban in 2012, I had a problem with my cell phone, and I went to nearby Lucena City, the capital of Quezon Province, to get the phone fixed. While there, it was necessary to cross the street to go to the phone repair store. However, there was a funeral procession happening, and it was necessary to wait for the traffic to pass before crossing the street. This was a parade with loudspeakers, a flatbed truck with a band playing funeral music, small children in costumes, and a large number of people marching in orderly fashion. After the flatbed truck passed, those who were following that parade were chanting and weeping very loudly. This was a very impactful event that I will never forget. It was much different from any funeral I have experienced in Canada.

Golfing in Paradise at Lipa City

After the assignment at SLSU in 2014, I went to Lipa City and joined my family where we spent a few days at the Mount Marayat Golf Course Resort. Because of my wife's connection to that country, our family had an inside track on where to travel what to see. We are able to recruit Clarita's brother Artemio, commonly called June, to be our driver and protector. He lives in the Philippines, and he was happy to look after his sister's family. When in the Philippines, we can travel very cheaply. We felt comfortable with June, and he is a great guy.

Lipa City was about a two-hour drive from Lucban. While staying at the Mount Marayat Golf Course resort, June and I played couple of rounds on the course. I am not the world's greatest golfer for sure, but that course was the most magnificent I have ever seen in my life, with beautiful coconut and palm trees and lush vegetation. We played thirty-six holes of golf over two days. This was not an Indiana Jones adventure since, because in order to play on that course, we were required to use a golf cart and hire a caddy. Those caddies carried our clubs, gave advice on what club to use for each shot, and teed-up golf balls for us—we were not allowed to do that ourselves. I recall playing one of those holes where I needed to drive my ball about 150 yards over a pond to get to the green. I played it like Kevin Costner did in the movie Tin Cup - and drove eight straight balls into the pond. I overestimated myself and made a fool of myself for sure.

Lucban in the Rear View Mirror

Both of my trips to Lucban in the Philippines – in 2012, and then the return visit for another assignment in 2014, were very nice. This is a smaller community and very safe. It took only one day to feel comfortable while there. The hospitality, customer service and helpfulness of everyone I encountered during my two trips was extraordinary. Filipinos really know how to celebrate and have a good time, without the noticeable rowdiness and drunkenness often seen in other places. I made some long-lasting friendships. I was always treated with great respect.

Most definitely Lucban is one of my favourite places in the Philippines.

FOOTNOTES

1. Census of the Philippines, Encyclopedia Britannica (copyright 2020), as cited in Wikipedia
2. Census of the Philippines, Encyclopedia Britannica (copyright 2020) as cited in Wikipedia, and Statistics Canada comparative figures for British Columbia, Canada

Pictures of Lucban, Philippines, and Field Trips for the CESO Project

From top left: CESO Tourism Assignment; Lucban central plaza; Weekly worker ceremony; Statue of Philippine hero; Landfill sorting and composting; Landfill composted product; Reclaiming the landfill; Organic farming at OISCA; Organic farming at Costales Farm; Rice planting with the Caribao; Hospitality at a Filipino home; Coconut harvest

Pictures of Lucban, Philippines, and Field Trips for the CESO Project

From top left: Jepnay; Tricycles; Kamay Ni Jesus – stairway to heaven; The beauty contest; San Luis De Tolosa Cathedral; Bakla – Master of Ceremonies; Watching the Manny Pacquio fight; Lucban Christmas party – 1970s theme; Lucban Christmas party band; CESO Training – Tourism Action Plan 2012; Panel on Climate Change; CESO Workshop SLSU 2014; PNEE Conference 2014

From top left: Pahiyas Festival; Pahiyas Festival; Mount Malarayat Golf Course; SLSU instructors 2014; Cultural Dance; Cultural Dance; Lucban landfill workers; Lucban Municipal Office; Restaurant on the water; Lucban noodle factory; Lucban Longganisa sausage factory

Chapter 3

THE PHILIPPINES

Encounters with Typhoons and Tropical Storms

Pexels.com- free stock photos

The Powerful Reality of the Philippines

Before I carry on telling the stories of other CESO assignments and travel adventures, I need to describe the everyday reality of scary encounters with dangerous weather, the rainy season, tropical storms, and typhoons. These situations are often unpredictable and life threatening, and I learned this firsthand. My first two assignments in San Pedro Sula, Honduras and Lucban, Philippines, were at inland locations, and while there, I did not experience the extreme danger one can encounter in coastal areas or at sea. In this chapter I will describe some scary and near life-threatening incidents at sea, never to be forgotten.

Alabat Island – In the Shadow of Typhoon Haiyan in 2013

My third CESO volunteer assignment in the Philippines was on Alabat Island and it began with some tension right from the start. A super typhoon, Typhoon Haiyan (referred to as Typhoon Yolanda in Asia) struck the Philippines on November 8, 2013. An estimated 6,350 people are thought to have died and one million homes destroyed in the central Philippine province of Leyte due to this typhoon, one of the strongest storms ever recorded. [1] It lashed out, swallowing coastal towns in the area, with Tacloban City being almost totally destroyed. I was scheduled to undertake a CESO project on November 10, but after hearing of the shocking events, I contacted the CESO Toronto office to see if it was still safe to travel to the Philippines. Apparently, the weather was okay in Luzon (the largest, northern island), but not in the central Visayas region, where the severe damage occurred. They told me that traveling to the Philippines and to Alabat Island should be okay. As far as the CESO 2013 assignment, it proceeded on schedule, with heavy rainfall and strong winds but without too many problems. (Details of the Alabat assignments are included in the next chapter.) The typhoon's epi-centre was only about 300 kilometers away from the town of Alabat. Although the weather conditions were inconvenient and not desirable, it was not an impediment to completing the work for that project.

Meeting a Lady Returning to a Devastated Family Home in the Philippines

At the beginning of my trip, as I waited in Vancouver for the connecting Philippine flight to Manila, and eventually enroute to Alabat Island, I spoke to a Filipino lady, who had recently become a Canadian citizen. She was flying back to her country of origin to bring her five-year-old son to live with her in Winnipeg, Canada. She was from Rojas City near the area of typhoon destruction. The news was devastating for her. This lady was unable to contact her son and her mother, who was looking after him. Upon arrival in Manila, she was again beside me as we picked up our baggage from the carousel. She told me the commercial flights to Tacloban City or Rojas City were all cancelled. I asked the CESO driver who picked me up if we could help her and take her to a hotel near the airport, and he was happy to do it. I never heard any more about her situation after that. I hope she and her family were okay. I will never forget that incident. That was my first awareness of typhoons and the hardship they cause to people in the Philippines.

Typhoon Amang Near Alabat Island in 2015

I returned to Alabat Island for a second time for a follow-up CESO assignment in January 2015. That project was impacted by another typhoon incident. It takes four-and-a-half hours to drive from Manila to the port at Atimonan, and from there you need to take a forty-five-minute Roro (ferry service) to Alabat Island. Within days of my arrival, there was severe weather warning about Typhoon Amang (also referred to locally as Typhoon Mekkhala). That storm, I was told, killed three people in the nearby Bicol Region, not far from Alabat Island, and it also caused widespread crop damage. Notably, the storm disturbed the touring schedule of Pope Francis, who was visiting the country at that time. However, I was able to get my picture taken with Pope Francis at the Catholic Church (or could it have been his cardboard replica). I will never tell! It may have been the Pope who kept me safe during that typhoon, even though I am not of the catholic religion.

Tailgating with the The Emergency Response Team on Alabat Island

I had direct exposure to the emergency planning operation taking place in 2015. The typhoon warning caused great panic on Alabat Island. The local Incident Command Centre was put into high alert. People living along the coastline were evacuated in anticipation of storm surges, potential loss of lives, and property destruction. Mayor Mesa and his wife Vangie took me in the municipal truck along the coastline. The local government unit (LGU) officials coaxed many people out of their mostly flimsy coastal homes, and they jumped into the municipal trucks with a few belongings. Then they were delivered to the local schools, where they stayed for at least the duration of the storm. I went with Mayor Mesa and Vangie to the school and saw many of the families crowded in those classrooms. There were bamboo coverings and thin floor mats on the concrete floors, no beds. That is where the families would sleep. I was surprised at how calm those families were. When they saw me—the only foreign Caucasian on Alabat Island at that time, many in the room wanted a picture taken with me, along with the mayor and his wife. The small children ran up to me and hugged my leg. What an adventure that was. Travelling amid a typhoon, watching evacuations, and seeing the command centre in operation—it was scary but exciting to watch how everyone performed so well under pressure.

Resilient Filipinos

Typhoons and tropical storms are a way of life in the Philippines. People seem to adjust, carry-on, and continue doing things, as if whatever happens is "God's will." My level of panic and stress was usually much greater than theirs. During Typhoon Amang, kids were playing basketball, and men were planting rice in the fields during heavy the winds and rain. That was very surprising for me to observe. The Filipinos are resilient people

Travelling to Itbayat in the Province of Batanes

In July 2017, I was on a CESO assignment in the Batanes islands, which are seven islands off the northern coast of Luzon. The islands are located in-between Luzon Island and Taiwan. Again, I found myself amid the rainy season, typhoons, and other bad elements. After the previous encounters with the turbulent weather, you would think I would have been more cautious. But just like an Indiana Jones movie, an unexpected adventure happened again. Three of the Batanes islands are inhabited, Batan, Sabtang, and Itbuyet. Batan and Sabtang are close together, and these were visited and investigated with little difficulty. Itbuyet is a three-and-a-half to five-hour boat ride from the town of Basco on Batan island, depending on the weather conditions. The other travel alternative would have been to take a military flight from Basco to Itbuyet Island.

In doing this CESO assignment, I wanted to be sure I would get first-hand experience with all of the habitable islands of the province of Batanes, so I expressed a desire to go to Itbuyet as well. This trip turned out to be a frightening and life-threatening experience. My god, I will never forget that day. Arrangements had been initially made for me to accompany the military on a flight to Itbuyet at ten o'clock in the morning. At seven o'clock there was a knock on the door, and I was told the military flight was cancelled due to a tropical storm, so I would have to leave right away and take the boat service, since the boat ride would take much longer. I was a little reluctant, but because this was the only chance, I would have to see Itbuyet island, I agreed.

The Perfect Storm – the Scariest Encounter of my Life

Breakfast was eaten on the run, and we boarded the boat. It was raining hard. The first half hour was a bit rough but not too bad. After that, all hell broke loose in the open sea. It was just like the movie "The Perfect Storm", starring George Clooney. I have never seen anything like that in my life. After all, I am a small-town boy, raised in Manitoba on the Canadian prairies—rough oceans are not my thing. There was a five-storey wave wall of water on either side of the boat, and we were rocking and rolling to the extreme. To this day, I do not know how I survived the ordeal. But I did pay a heavy price. After half an hour of leaving the port at Basco, my breakfast decided it wanted to be in the ocean. I had to go to the back of the boat, where there was no cover from the pouring rain. With the rocking and rolling, I threw up continually for the better part of two hours. I was totally wet from being in the rain. Others on the boat were sick too, but I seemed to be in the roughest shape. Well, we made it to the landing point at Itbayat. I thought the ordeal was over. Not quite.

Getting Off the Boat at Itbuyet Island—Another Scary Moment

The boat had to dock, but there was no dock, just a ledge carved out of the shoreline rock. The boatmen tied the boat to the shore with long ropes, but the boat was moving up and down, it seemed to be in thirty-to-forty-foot swells. There were fierce winds blowing. Three strong men on the shore waited for the boat to rock up to the point where it was even with the ledge. They grabbed each passenger's arms in turn, and then pulled all the passengers from the boat to the ledge quickly as the boat rolled up and down. If their grip failed, the passenger would drop and hit the rocky shore below, where they would either die of the impact with the rocky shoreline or be drowned in the ocean. I think there were about forty of us onboard that boat, and we were all pulled to shore safely. The driver of that boat and those three men on the shore were amazing.

Rough Seas and Another Tropical Storm—Island Hopping Near El Nido

Philippine weather can be frightening. After completing the assignment in Batanes, my family—Claire, Riley, Dylan, and Danika and I—travelled to Palawan, a large island on the western side of the Philippines. We went "island hopping" and enjoyed small islands off the coast of Palawan. We stopped at a beautiful tropical island near El Nido and did some snorkeling, and then went ashore at a secluded bay. We had a magnificent feast of seafood, meats, vegetables, fruits, noodles, and tropical juices, all provided as part of the tour. It was incredible, until as we departed, another ugly tropical storm arrived yet again. A bunch of tour-guided boats decided to hold-up and shelter by the small island for an hour or two until the storm passed. However, out of the seventeen boats that were waiting out the storm and the rough seas, two guide boats decided to cross the open seas to return to El Nido without waiting. Wouldn't you know it, our boat was one of them. We were a family of five, Clarita's brother June, and the boatmen. Well, I would say it was not as bad as the trip to Itbuyet Island a few weeks earlier, but it was very bad. There was a tent-like canopy shade over the top of the boat, and as we hit the open seas, the winds ripped it off. We were no longer sheltered from the heavy rain, and as a result, for the rest of the journey returning to El Nido, we got totally soaked in the rain. The smaller boat was rocking and rolling, but the driver guide did an excellent job and jig-jagged his way, negotiating the big waves quite effectively. We returned to El Nido successfully.

Typhoon Disaster in the Philippine Sea at Polillo Island

There was another incident related to the treacherous weather in the Philippines, that involved my Filipino friend Edling Tallisayon. I was on Polillo Island doing three CESO projects from August 9 – September 4, 2015. I travelled on the large ferry boat which connected the towns on Polillo Island to the city of Real, which is situated on the main island of Luzon. I did not have major problems travelling by boat during my visit to that island. However, Edling was the Planning and Development Coordinator for Burdeos LGU on Polillo Island and I worked closely with him during one week in the Burdeos area. I ate several meals with his family at their home. While back in Canada about two years later, on December 17, 2017, I was informed that Edling was on the same Mercraft 3 boat which I had travelled on to get to Polillo Island. It capsized during stormy weather with 258 people on board, and ninety-two people drowned. Fortunately, Edling was a survivor, although he was hospitalized for some time because of that event. The Mercraft 3 was also the same marine vessel which I traveled on when going from Basco to Itbayat, while in the Batanes islands, in the summer of 2017. My friend did survive, but that incident was a "wake-up call" – life is short.

The Frightening Typhoons and Tropical Storms of the Philippines in the Rear View Mirrow

If one is to travel on the open seas near the Philippines, it helps to be like Indiana Jones—prepared for some adventure, potential danger, and irregular schedules. I was not anticipating the drama and danger involved in the inter-island travel throughout the Philippines. I can now say I have had experiences where I was a way out of my comfort zone. I can honestly say, I was living on the edge on a few occasions. Filipinos experience these risks as a matter of course, as so many live on more isolated islands and need to travel to the larger island centers from time-to-time.

Would I travel in those Filipino boats during rough weather in those open seas? Do I want to encounter tropical storms or typhoons again? No thanks . . . I have had enough of that.

FOOTNOTES

1. Kenneth Pletcher and John P. Rafferty, <u>Super Typhoon Haiyan Storm: Northern Pacific Ocean (2013)</u> Encyclopedia Britannica (2020); article cited in Wikipedi

Pictures Taken During Typhoons and Tropical Storms

From top left: Alabat Island evacuation of fisherfolk from coastal area; Mayor Mesa, Vangie and I with evacuated children; Alabat incident command centre; Rice planting during Typhoon Amang – Alabat Island; Kids playing basketball during storm; Alabat Island Weather Station; Travelling to Itbuyet Island during typhoon; Pope Francis Philippine visit 2015; Extremely steep shoreline at Itbuyet Island; Exiting the boat on Itbuyet Island; Departing with Life Jackets on board; Rough seas near Polillo Island

Chapter 4

THE PHILIPPINES

Assignments in Alabat Island and the Polillo
Group of Islands Between 2013 and 2019

Map prepared by Lance Smith
Chapter 4 Map –

Two Island Areas in Quezon Province—
Similar CESO Assignments

In working in the Philippines and completing work in Lucban, I had developed a connection with Matt Navalta, the CESO CR, as well as some of the local area clients for whom I had worked. Matt was perhaps the most organized CESO country representative I worked with in all my assignments, and he became a good friend. He was also a talented karaoke singer and musician. I believe this connection and friendship with Matt and his assistant Erwin Altamarino and the general success of my projects in the Philippines, helped me to be recruited for other assignments there.

Two of the earlier assignment opportunities were on more remote islands on the south and eastern side of Luzon (the main island) in Quezon Province, within the Philippine Sea. Alabat Island is a singular island. The Polillo Group of Islands consists of twenty-seven islands, the three most populated being Polillo, Patnanugan and Jomilig. There were five LGU's (local government units established for local government administration), three of which were on the largest main island being Polillo Island.

Alabat Island in the Philippines

Alabat Island consists of three LGU's which contain a population of about 42,000 people. It has an area of 192 square kilometers or 92 square miles. [1] It is a beautiful tropical island located about 200 kilometers south of Manila, but it also involves travelling five or six hours by a *Roro* ferry to get there. People are mostly engaged in agriculture and fishing. The area does not receive many tourists, although it does have potential for tourism, particularly due to its pristine environment, the natural beauty, and the agricultural assets of the area.

The CESO Assignment on Alabat Island

During my time as a CESO volunteer, I completed five assignments in three trips to Alabat Island, in 2013, 2015, and 2019.

The 2013 CESO assignment required the completion of Integrated Comprehensive Development Plans for three LGU's on Alabat Island—Alabat,

Quezon, and Perez. I was eminently qualified for this project, as this was the type of work I did regularly as a city planner in different Canadian cities for over thirty years. Upon arriving in Alabat, I immediately met with the three mayors of those LGU's and their staff officials. Because the assignment required integrated plans, it was a little more complicated and more intense than the usual single-client assignments. It was a four-week project, and I needed to work a near equal amount of time in each municipality. This work focused on the key issues of concern, developing a common approach for each LGU so that they were coordinated in their sustainable economic development and environmental management approaches. The workload was heavy, but the cooperation and coordination from everyone was terrific. There were some issues—a three-day power outage during the storm, loss of the internet, and loss of some data. Despite that, I was able to complete the work in four weeks, and the results were well received. I was told these were the first integrated plans undertaken in Quezon Province and few of these types of plans had been done elsewhere in the country. It was a privilege to have had that opportunity.

Through this work with all the field trips, meetings, and venturing out for dinner with friends, there were new lessons learned, and some Indiana Jones – types of adventures. Who has heard of Alabat Island anyway? Well, I have stories to tell.

Lambanog

During my 2012 assignment in Lucban, I had an opportunity to taste the local moonshine called *Lambanog*. It is made from either coconuts or Nipa fruits which come from mangrove palm trees. I went on a field trip on a lengthy trail on Alabat Island where I was able to see a home-made "still" (distillery). These guys, in a remote part of the forest, really knew how to make *Lambanog*. They provided a sample. The true test was demonstrated when the distilled lambanog on a rock and lit a match to it. Apparently, if it lit on fire, you knew you had a good batch of Lambanog. Well, let us just say that it was a good batch. My motorcycle driver and I tasted it—very, very strong—and I bought some with me to Canada in a large-sized Coke bottle. It has now been consumed, but I am not sure how many brain cells were destroyed from consuming that very potent substance.

CESO Assignment—Integrated Comprehensive Development Plans for LGU's on Alabat Island

This CESO assignment required me to investigate the economy of Alabat Island. That included looking at the economic, social, and environmental management conditions, as well as the infrastructure in the LGU's. In the Philippines, the social structure and local culture were especially important, and understanding these were particularly necessary to formulate economic and environmental strategies.

Agriculture Production

Agriculture is a key to the future of Alabat Island and the Philippines in general, and there are many crops harvested there. In the Philippines, rice is eaten with every meal. Rice or *pilay* is grown methodically and consistently year-after-year, two crops per year. I went out in the field and experienced the harvest in progress. I also saw rice drying on mats in front of houses, and on roadways. Vehicles respect the need for this and navigate around the mats in their vehicles and motorcycles. There is no concern with traffic management. That is just what people do there, an everyday practice.

Throughout Quezon Province, coconut production is huge. I took a turn harvesting coconuts, knocking them down from the tree with a thirty-foot bamboo pole. You must be careful when the coconuts fall like bombs from the sky because they could kill you. An alternative harvesting method is to climb the tall trees and cut them down with a machete—no thanks! Between 2013 and 2019, I witnessed the coconut farming transformed from the harvesting of the coconut fruits from the trees in the wild, to farming a genetically engineered variety. *Macupuno* is being now being planted. It is a higher yield, higher quality coconut now harvested for greater economic input.

The AIFPC—The Alabat Island Farmers Producers Cooperative—2019 CESO Assignment

In 2019, I did an assignment to assist a newly formed organization, the AIFPC—Alabat Island Farmers Producers Cooperative, to prepare a new strategic plan for improved agricultural processes, higher levels of production, and the marketing of certain agricultural products. This group also worked closely with Alabat Island's Mayor Mesa. New markets for exporting specialty crops were found in Southern Luzon and in Manila. The crops being exported included chili peppers, calamansi (a citrus fruit), cassava, bananas for chips and coconut. Local wine (Lipote) was made from locally grown blackberries and this new enterprise involved exporting off-island in 2019. I was impressed as this was an exceptionally high-quality wine.

The Villa Marcelina Cacao Farm

I visited the Villa Marcelina Cacao Farm outside of Alabat in 2015, and then again in 2019. Cacao is a raw form of chocolate, and I drank it freshly harvested. It was a wonderful experience. It was fantastic seeing the trees with the cacao fruits, harvesting of the plants, preparing the cacao, and drinking it. On my last trip to Alabat in 2019, I was saddened to hear from Nora Marcelina that her husband, who I had pictures of from 2015, had recently passed away. I remembered him from that visit. He was a truly kind man.

Camagong Mountain

Camagong Mountain is the highest mountain and most dominant landscape on Alabat Island. The client hosts took me to Villa Norte, located on the coast of the Philippine Sea of the Pacific Ocean on the eastern side of that island. It is a picturesque remote village at the end of the road. At Villa Norte, we then began a six-kilometer hike to Bosay Falls at the base of the mountain. Soon after we began our hike, it started to rain, and the trail turned to mud. It was safer to try to walk on the side of the trail and avoid slipping and sliding in the mud. A sloppy start to the day for sure, but in a few hours the rain stopped, and the hiking was easier.

There were spots where people lived along that remote trail. No vehicles could access the area, so goods and supplies were delivered by donkeys with side-saddles, or by horses hauling small trailers. In the remote area of the jungle, I also saw fishermen building their own boats using pandan leaves and bamboo from the jungle forest - it was intriguing to see that level of craftsmanship. A skill passed down for generations. This hike was so informative, and it was like travelling back in time 100 years!

It was a long journey, but we finally reached Bosay Falls, and they were spectacular. As beautiful as they were, though, along the beach and beside the falls when the tide was out, the beach was covered in plastic and other debris. What a contrast—the natural beauty of the remote area, and then the large volumes of garbage which had accumulated on the beach. This was washed ashore from thousands of miles away. That is the sad state of our oceans, the reality of our world now.

The hike up to Camagong Mountain was difficult and steep. My host guides gave me some advice before the climb— "Watch out for the green snakes. If they bite you, in three minutes you die . . . but it is unlikely we will encounter them." Wow, that was not very comforting! So, we started to climb. Well, in my younger years ago I was a sports guy in good condition, but I soon realized that I was not in very good shape anymore! That was a tough climb. Thankfully, I made it up the mountain and we had good fortune that day to not see any green snakes.

Dining the Traditional Filipino Way at Villa Norte— Boddle Fight

After the hike we returned to Villa Norte, and after that workout, the group of us who were hiking were extremely hungry. The return hike was another six kilometers, much of it was climbing, so that was a tiring day. The meal was "boddle fight," Filipino style with no plates or utensils—you eat with your hands with banana leaves underneath. We enjoyed a meal of grilled fish and jellyfish (that was weird, but tasted ok), and rice. After our meal, we walked through the village and found some local fishermen returning from a day at sea with two huge yellow fin tuna, as well as smaller *lapu lapu* (grouper) and sea bass. Those tuna were, I'm guessing, forty or fifty pounds. I wish I had caught one of those beautiful tuna—wow!

A Drunken Fisherman

While on Alabat Island in 2013, I was invited for dinner at a home, with the hosts while in the LGU of Perez. After supper, karaoke was being sung and, on the street, neighbours nearby began to dance. It was Saturday night, and a man came up to me and suggested I dance with his wife, and he danced with one of the host ladies. He was quite drunk, loud, and slurring his words in Tagalog. It felt uncomfortable and awkward for me, but I danced. As the karaoke and dancing ended, my hosts told me that this man was a fisherman who he went fishing for 16 hours a day for 6 days a week. Every Saturday night, he got drunk. Sunday was his day of rest. They said he is a harmless, hardworking man, and he was entitled to his preferred Saturday night of pleasure.

Touring Protected Fish Sanctuaries and Fish Cages (Fish Farms)

My terrific Alabat hosts took me on a wonderful boat tour of the shoreline to view an environmentally protected marine and fish sanctuary. They also took me snorkeling on a coral reef, and it was quite amazing. A local diver brought to the surface a giant clam, locally called *taklobo*, and it was huge. Because it is a protected species, the diver gave us a few minutes to take pictures, and then returned it to the sea. We also encountered a fisherman who had caught an octopus, which was not a protected species. My hosts bought it, and we ate it at the mayor's house that evening for supper. They knew how to cook it properly, and it tasted delicious.

Mayor Fernando Mesa—A Great Leader

I first met Mayor Fernando Mesa of Alabat LGU in 2013, and he is one of the most inspirational leaders I have ever seen. I am so inspired how he leads his people, and how fond of him they are. I have been amazed at the things he accomplishes for his people, and how he gets action in a short period of time. In spending time with him, I was able to observe him in action, putting his people first, and always striving to solve problems and make things better. He is not just a man who reacts but a man with vision, stated repeatedly in his own words, "to uplift the lives of the people on Alabat Island." He has certainly done that during his years as mayor, and I am proud to call Fernando my friend.

Fernando was in the Philippine Army during his life, he climbed the ranks, and eventually becoming a general. He was wounded three times in combat, and he received high honors in military service. While in the hospital, he met his wife Vangie. They have been married for several decades. In his work as mayor, she is often by his side and she is a trusted confidant, making a valuable contribution to the office. They are an effective team. While in the military, Fernando also served as a high-level military envoy in Europe and in North America, and I am certain that military training was instrumental in Fernando's focus and emphasis on results. Visions, policies, and ideas are not simply to be talked about, they are to be implemented, and in Alabat, he has done just that.

National Focus on Law and Order—Philippine President Rodrico Dutarte

On the national scale, since the induction of Rodrico Dutarte as the new president of the Philippines in June 2016, there has been a strong "law and order" emphasis in the government platform. I observed this on my later travels to the Philippines in 2017 and 2019. Since 2016, I saw a proliferation of billboards promoting law and order, in Quezon Province and other areas in the Philippines. The emphasis on stopping corruption, the war against illegal drugs, and attempts to defeat the Abu Sabaya rebels in Mindinao in the southern Philippines was quite apparent. The president has openly applauded vigilante actions in support of his priorities, although his rhetoric and approach are not appreciated by democratic governments and human rights groups internationally. That said, in interfacing with Filipino people both in the Philippines and in Canada, I have observed almost overwhelming support expressed for the president and his actions. In Canada, we do not seem to support such an authoritarian style of government. Filipinos have felt overwhelmed by unruly and corrupt governments for decades. Under Mr. Dutarte, Filipinos I have met suggest that these issues are finally being addressed. There are two sides to every story, I guess.

Pictures of Alabat Island and Field Trips

From top left: CESO Assignment – Inter-municipal planning; Mayor Mesa of Alabat Island addressing audience; Coconut Harvest with pole; Rice harvest step #1; Rice harvest step #2; Rice harvest step #3; Macupuno – Genetically modified coconut; Bosay Falls; The cacao farm; Transporting goods by horse – Vila Norte trail; A mud trail to Bosay Falls; Coastal area pollution

Pictures of Alabat Island and Field Trips

From top left: Hiking up Camagong Mountain; Camagong Mountain; Boddle fight – eating with your hands; Cooking jellyfish; Taklobo – endangered giant clam; Fishermen with large tuna catch; Octopus; Lambanoc distillery; Road sign – Philippine war on drugs; New coconut sugar factory in Alabat – 2019; Mother bathing child at a water pump; Boat at the port – Alabat

About the Polillo Group of Islands

After completing integrated comprehensive development plans for Alabat Island as a CESO assignment in 2013, I was subsequently recruited by CESO to do the same project for the Polillo Group of Islands (POGI) in 2015. POGI has five local government units, twenty-seven islands, and a population of about 65,000. [2] No other CESO assignments had ever been undertaken on Polillo Island before, so perhaps I should have known more Indiana Jones adventures would be forthcoming. I knew this would be a huge undertaking, but I agreed to go for four weeks in August and September 2015. There was a lot of similarity in issues facing the remote islands in the Philippines, and with the experience of previous assignments there, I felt confident in doing the work.

Travelling to Polillo Island

Travelling from Canada to Manila was, as usual, long and tiring, but it went quite smoothly with no real surprises. I was picked up by a driver after spending the night at a Manila hotel near the airport. My recollection of this trip includes venturing through the heavy congestion and pollution in Metro-Manila and several hours of driving to the Port at Real. This is a city on the east coast of the main island of Luzon. A nice drive but very windy, and I recall feeling car-sick before getting to port. The hosts had a solution for me—we stopped for food, and they suggested I eat *arroz caldo* (like Chinese congee). Now that was a tremendous solution. The rice soup with ginger and garlic coated my stomach, and in about ten minutes, I was feeling fine. After about four hours of traveling from Manila, the next step was to take the *Roro* (ferryboat) from Port at Real to the town of Polillo, which took another three hours. This went well. The ocean was calm. Upon arriving, I was taken to a nice hotel.

The First Supper on Polillo Island—It was Napakasarap (delicious)

At the hotel, the host provided CESO Assistant CR Vener Velario and me a spectacular seafood meal that consisted of crabs, shrimp, fish, and *laing*—taro grows wild in many areas, and they are used for *laing*, which includes chili peppers, onions, garlic, and coconut sauce. Oh my god, a meal could not get any better than that! I am not sure whether Anthony Bourdain ever ate *laing*? I think he would have liked it.

CESO Workshops for Integrated Development Plans on Polillo Island

I have to say, the actual work I did in Polillo, and later in Burdeos and Panukulan, were interesting and remarkable in terms of the intensive participation, interest, and input received for the project. For many of the projects I had done in the Philippines, the people seemed to listen more than speak. The most common attitude I encountered was, "Sir, you are the expert, tell us what to do." The Polillo Island folks were quite assertive, and comments and opinions were freely expressed. That was good—it gave credibility to the project and helped in the achievement of formulating well thought out, relevant, integrated plans for the three municipalities. This would truly be their plan.

The Southern Polillo Island Field Trip

My Polillo hosts took me on a one-day voyage to investigate some of the further out islands. This would help me to gain greater understanding of the project and the long-term plans and recommendations to be developed. Although it was background for the work, it was another travel adventure. I think tourists would dream about such an experience. Although this was a five-hour boat ride each way, much of the route was along the Polillo Island shoreline, stopping occasionally. It was calm at sea. We stopped at Bata Beach, the location of remnants of an old port which had been constructed by the Japanese during the Second World War. We continued, along the shoreline of Patnanugan Island. We went ashore at Minasawa Island, although no people were living there because it was a bird sanctuary. This was a long and enjoyable trip for the eight people on board. Many things were observed, and stories were exchanged. We returned to the town of Polillo just in time to view a beautiful sunset. What a momentous day!

The Pregnant Women's Talent Contest

Just when I thought I that I understood the life in this area, another surprise. Mayor Bosque from Polillo knocked on my door at the hotel and said, "I am taking you to an exciting event tonight." This was not on the agenda, but I thought, why not! It was a pregnant women's talent contest. At the show, many of these women were extremely pregnant, on stage, singing, dancing, or doing stand-up comedy acts. Wow— I had never seen anything quite so strange before, but most of those women were extremely well prepared, quite attractive despite their condition and extremely talented. It was a very entertaining evening, and hilarious. There were a lot of people in attendance -nearly the whole town of Polillo I think. Everyone went home happy.

Harvesting Seaweed

Another field trip took place with The Polillo Island Agriculture Department who showed me the harvesting process for one of their major exports from the sea—seaweed. The centre for this harvesting was about a twenty-minute boat ride from the town of Polillo, a cottage anchored in the water on stilts. The man in charge demonstrated a lot of skill in retrieving seaweed from the ocean. It was a primitive operation, but skillfully done and that is the way they did it.

The Electric Power Shortage Affecting Polillo Island

In Polillo, I met with the Napacor power company officials during my CESO assignment. I learned that all the electrical power for Polillo Island was generated from six diesel generators. I was not allowed to take pictures inside that facility, but three of the six generators were not working due to mechanical failures. Replacement of workable parts was required. These repairs were difficult and expensive, I was told. Due to this problem, the power had to be shut down on a Polillo Island for twelve hours every day! This was an inconvenient situation for those on Polillo Island, and for me. It was an extremely hot climate, and because power was off for most of the night, no air-conditioning was possible. Instead of electricity, the locals survived with kerosene lamps or candles. They cooked with *copra* (charcoal made from coconut shells). The locals accustomed to the climate, and air-conditioning was not so necessary for them. These folks simply adjusted, and most did not even complain. The electronic devices were only used during the day.

Napacor did not seem to be in a rush to replace those generator parts. I expressed my opinion with the Napacor manager, that it might be better if more green energy solutions including solar and wind power might replace those polluting diesel systems in the future. He nodded but suggested that was a decision others would make.

Travelling from the town of Polillo to the town of Burdeos on Polillo Island

After one week in the town of Polillo, I departed for the town of Burdeos. They sent me with two drivers on two smaller motorcycles, 125cc. I knew these machines well, as many years ago I used to have a 100cc motorcycle growing up in Manitoba. The two motorcycle drivers and I travelled ninety minutes on some rough gravel roads. I was a passenger on one motorcycle, and the other driver took my luggage on his motorcycle. This journey was a bit wild by my usual standards, but Indiana Jones would have appreciated this method of travelling. This mode of transportation would be repeated on my next leg of the trip one week later, travelling from Burdeos to Panukulan.

Burdeos and the Assignment Field Trip

We made it safely to the town of Burdeos, a small community of only a few thousand people within a large-sized municipality. In Burdeos, I felt lost and so far away from everywhere, but the people were very welcoming. On the first day, I was taken on an island-hopping excursion to view parts of that the local area and get an overview of the social, environmental, and economic conditions as part of the assignment background. We had a full day of seeing things. After a twenty-minute boat ride, we came to a protected conservation area. My hosts showed me a Philippine brown deer, which I was told was on the International Union of Conservation of Nature list for endangered species. We then pro-ceeded down a trail to an area with caverns or caves with icicle formations called stalactites and stalagmites. They were remarkable, but another Indiana Jones moment happened here. The cavern area, as it turned out, was vertical and not horizontal. I threw a stone down the hole and there was no sound, so I think it was a bottomless "black hole." The hosts asked me to come and walk along a narrow ledge and go to the other side of the cavern for a better view. My guides for the day, Edling and his cousin Ronan, told me to follow them along this edge path beside the vertical cavern—I was wearing flip flops! I started to follow them down this path, and it got narrower and narrower until it was thirty to forty centimeters wide. My flip-flops were not very secure, and it was slippery. I looked down into that dark hole and panicked. "Help me. I cannot go any further." It took them about three minutes to reach me, and I was shaking at the edge. They took me to safety, unharmed. It was an extremely scary moment for me.

Remote Island Hopping and the Pearl Farm

We left the sanctuary and travelled to another beautiful island. There was a fantastic meal prepared for us on the spectacular beach—fresh grilled yellow tuna, prawns, rice, and fresh mangos. After we ate, they wanted to show me a pearl harvesting farm, in a secluded bay area on another island, two hours away. At that location, oysters were shucked, and pearls were retrieved in the processing. We visited this facility, but there was no one working that day. I was told the pearls harvested from this facility were sold and exported to Japan.

Local Ingenuity Using Alternate Energy

As with the Town of Polillo, Burdeos was also subject to power rationing. Edling, who I worked with in Burdeos, as I mentioned earlier, became a good friend of mine. I had a few dinners at his home with his family. This guy was not just somebody who had ideas, but he made them happen. Edling had a self-reliant solution to the power shortage situation at his home. He installed a small solar panel. In addition to that, he used waste from the hogs on his small farm, combined with plant waste and this produced biogas, which was then used for family cooking. Through his alternate energy, he could be off the grid and not need to use power from the utility company at all.

Travelling from Burdeos to Panukulan

My next stop in the 2015 Polillo Island CESO assignment was Panukulan, on the northern side of the island. The travelling from Burdeos to Panukulan turned into yet another adventure. I was told on the last evening spent in Burdeos that I was to be picked up at ten o'clock, but again, there was a knock on my door saying that due to weather problems, they wanted me to leave after breakfast at seven and travel in the same fashion as a week earlier, by motorcycle. The timing would again be one and a half hours to go to a place called Binibitinan, where a boat would take me across a bay to Panukulan. The boat would take thirty to forty-five minutes, depending on the sea conditions. The travel to the village of Binibitinan went well enough on the dirt roads, but upon arriving at the port, there was nobody there to pick me up. The two motorbike drivers waited with me for an hour, but nobody came, and there was no cellphone service to allow us to call ahead. There was a main attraction while we waited—a man having a swim with horse. Such an event was new to me, but it was entertaining.

Finding Another Way to Get to Panukulan—Did They Forget to Pick Me Up?

The local people informed us that there was a small fishing port about fifteen minutes distance by motorbike, and there might be someone there who could take me across to Panukulan. This would be a slightly shorter boat ride to Panukulan as well, so I agreed to this arrangement. My motorcycle drivers and I left, and we discovered the route to the port was a jungle trail not a road for most of the way. It was a very bumpy ride on a narrow pathway, and branches were constantly hitting our faces, but eventually we found the small port. It was simple and primitive looking, located in a channel flowing to the ocean. Because tide was out, boats were grounded, so I had to wait an additional hour before the boats could negotiate the channel and continue to the ocean. The motorbike drivers left, and suddenly I was afraid because of the uncertainty of my travel. "What the heck was I doing there?" "Was I ever going to get where I needed to be?" The boat driver was a very modest and simple person, he was missing some of his teeth, his boat was old, and he did not speak English, but he was a very decent guy. I trusted him. After paying him a proper amount to take me across the bay, and loading my luggage onto this small boat, we departed. It was a rough ride in the ocean, and I later found out that this was the reason for my delayed pickup. Unfortunately, the guy who went to pick me up had arrived in Binibitinan while I arrived in Panukulan. This was an unfortunate mix-up.

Panukulan turned out to be a beautiful town, and people were extremely hospitable. After settling in at my accommodation, I was picked up and taken to a special evening in my honour—the visitor from Canada. It was a very humbling and enjoyable evening. The mayor and top officials and business-people in the town attended. It was a big event, the food was again fantastic, with lots of seafood, which I loved. Of course, there was the opening prayer, Philippine anthem, lots of speeches, and karaoke. I was particularly impressed by Emma Ritual, who was the mayor's administrative assistant, who provided guidance and support to everyone. I noticed she always kept the mayor on track and ensured that high quality decisions were made. Emma was extremely competent and powerful. I suggested she should run to become a governor, senator, or become a congressperson, but she laughed at the idea. I thought she would do well in one of those roles, as she demonstrated tremendous leadership skills.

Field Trips Within Panukulan LGU

I was able to do some countryside field research throughout the Panukulan LGU, and there were some remarkable things to see. I experienced the rural life in this very remote island in the Philippines. Our travelling group was comprised of LGU officials, a doctor, and medical staff, who provided medical services throughout the area. The officials showed me infrastructure and other information for the CESO assignment. We took a small boat, travelled around the northern coastline of Polillo Island. We went to a small village, where the roads were like large sidewalks, about two meters wide, and severely cracked and in rough shape. These were used by pedestrians, motorcycles, and vehicles, and there were no lanes for passing. At this village, I observed young children and infants who were being inoculated. These places visited were very isolated, yet they were still connected to basic services provided to them.

Protection of the Environment on Polillo Island

From what I saw, most of Polillo Island is an undiscovered tropical paradise. It was so beautiful there. I did not encounter any foreigners (or any other Caucasians other than myself) during my stay there. I wonder how much longer this area will remain like this. It is difficult for foreigners to travel here, so perhaps this may keep this environmentally sensitive area intact for the foreseeable future. During the time of my visit, there was talk of United Nations through UNESCO declaring parts of Polillo Island as a National Heritage site. The Province of Quezon had already established local conservation areas on Polillo Island. An added UNESCO designation would be of major significance, but that would be the easy part. Despite such positive measures for protection of the biosphere, local enforcement would be needed so that the integrity of the area remains intact. With limited resources available, I am not sure that could be accomplished. The monitor lizards, the Philippine brown deer, and the *Taklobo* (giant clam) are inhabitants of the land and water of Polillo Island, and these species need protection. I am certain that there are many other animal, aquatic, and plant species, as well as landscapes needing protection in the pristine environment of Panukulan and throughout Polillo Island.

Amazing Perfume—*Ylang-Ylang*

I am told *ylang-ylang* leaves are the ingredient for the most expensive perfume in the world. While I was in the town of Panukulan, the streets were lined with the tree that produces *ylang-ylang*. I was visiting at the right time because as I walked down the streets, there was the most spectacular, pleasant aroma throughout the town. I was told the oil from *ylang –ylang* is harvested and sold to Japan where this perfume is in high demand.

Stingless Bees and Unique Honey

Have you ever heard of stingless bees? I noticed with curiosity that many houses in Panukulan had boat anchors hanging from the roof gutters of their houses. When I looked more closely, they were used as hives for stingless bees, common on islands in the Philippines. People did this as a source of their own honey, which tastes sour compared to regular honey. I tasted it, and it is very edible. This honey is also supposed to have medicinal benefits.

Departing From Polillo Island

It was time for me to leave Polillo Island. After this CESO assignment, I travelled from Panukulan to the port of Infanta by boat, and then to Lucena City, the capital of Quezon Province. This was again a full day of travel—three hours by boat, and then another four- or five-hour drive to Lucena City, where the final presentation and exit meeting for the project were to be held.

That boat ride was interesting. There was no port on the mainland of Luzon at Infanta and so, because the tide was out, the large ferry boat had to be moored about 250 meters from shore. Passengers were then lifted onto smaller boats, paddled closer to shore, and then it was time to take off the shoes and roll up the pant legs—if not wearing shorts—to walk about twenty-five meters to the shore in a few feet of water. I wish I had worn shorts and flip-flop sandals that day like many others did. It was an adventure to get to shore, as there was no proper docking facility, even though Infanta is a sizeable community of approximately 70,000 people.

The Exit Meeting and Discussions on Final Recommendations

After travelling from Infanta to Lucena City, after a night's rest, it was time for the CESO exit meeting and the final assignment presentation. In attendance was the CESO CR, mayors from five LGUs, politicians, and LGU staff. The final assignment presentation turned into an unanticipated battle. Three comprehensive development plans were completed for the local government units in Polillo, Burdeos, and Panukulan. A promise was made by myself and to CESO that I would return in three to six months and complete similar integrated plans for the other more distant LGUs at Patnanugan and Jomalig. The mayors from those two regions expressed disappointment that the comprehensive plans could not be completed within the next month or two, and before Christmas. Unfortunately, my time commitments back in Canada would not allow me to accommodate them. I felt bad about that, and unfortunately, those plans have never been completed.

There were issues in the plans completed that required some deep contemplation and healthy debate among the LGU officials present. During the public engagement sessions, many participants thought Polillo Island and POGI should become separated from Quezon province as a separate province in the Philippines. If not a separate province, an alternative would be having a separate congressional district established. Many felt that POGI issues were different from the rest of Quezon Province and other areas on the mainland of Luzon. Greater independence seemed like a promising idea to some. I understand the issue remains unresolved by those jurisdictions to this day. CESO does not, and should not involve itself in domestic politics - I was not going to do that.

Another issue was a discussion of the possible transfer of Minasawa Island from Burdeos LGU authority (four hours distance from the main island) to Patnanugan Island LGU authority (only thirty minutes from Minisawa Island). Closer surveillance, better protection, and enforcement regulations from an authority closer to that bird sanctuary seemed to be a better solution. The deputy mayor of Burdeos was not sure the council would support this, so she wanted this decision deferred. I understand the issue was resolved by those jurisdictions later, after assignment completion and my return to Canada.

I was so happy to hear that the three local government units all adopted the comprehensive plans at subsequent meetings after my departure, so this was a successful assignment. However, the LGUs of Patnanugan and Jomalig discontinued further participation in the integrated comprehensive development plan process. There was a scheduled follow-up assignment to the island LGUs of Patnanugan and Jomalig for the spring of 2016, but that did not happen. I guess you cannot win them all.

A Manila Incident—Be Careful at Night

Following this very challenging assignment, I was exhausted, and my hosts took me back to Manila, where I remained one day to rest before I was to fly back to Canada. I thought I had encountered enough adventure for one trip, but there was a very scary incident in Manila, which happened due to a bit of carelessness on my part. To be safe, I never went out at night. However, on that occasion I went for supper in the Robinson Mall in Malati, Manila at around five p.m. I forgot how fast it turns dark in the Philippines. The mall was located only one block from my hotel, and it was not a problem to walk there during the daytime. I exited that mall at about seven o'clock, it was very dark. The streets in the Philippines are not well lit.

I began to walk back to the hotel. About halfway, two small children aggressively grabbed my leg, and their mother was beside them with her hand out. She was begging for money. It was dark, I could barely move because of the children clutching my leg. Then a man came up to the other side of me and tried selling me some things including boxes of Viagra. I had bought a few things at the mall and was carrying a bag, and the man threw this Viagra into my bag, and he demanded that I pay him for it. I was being harassed from both sides in the dark, and walking was difficult. I felt like they were waiting for me to take my wallet out, and then one of them would snatch it. I was close to a street pole that had a very dim light. I did a quick twirl around the pole, then tossed the Viagra from my shopping bag back to that seller as I was twirling. I also got free from those children clutching my leg, and I ran the rest of the block back to the hotel as fast as I could. No harm done, but - what a narrow escape! I guess the spirit of Indiana Jones was with me that evening.

Alabat and the Polillo Group of Islands iin the Rear View Mirror

Filipinos work extremely hard and earn very little money by our standards in North America. I noticed the equipment the workers used was often old and not efficient. Substantial risk labour was the norm, without much regard for worker safety, in construction, transportation, and in other occupations. In the small rural towns, everyone knew everybody, and everyone seemed very happy and positive in their outlook, most believing that God would take care of them, no matter what happened.

More CESO opportunities in the Philippines were offered to me after 2015, and, the assignments were well received, which was very gratifying to me. I travelled throughout those wonderful islands, met many people, and experienced warm friendship and hospitality. I saw a lot of beautiful, beautiful areas during those visits to the Philippines. Alabat Island and the Polillo Group of Islands are true examples of rural island life in the Philippines, and they were both enjoyable and unforgettable experiences.

My concluding thoughts—if I had another opportunity to go back to Quezon Province in the Philippines, I would want to take full advantage and do that. The low cost of living, a beautiful natural landscape, a respectful culture, and friendly people - this made the visit to Quezon Province or anywhere in the Philippines a positive experience.

FOOTNOTES

1. Census of the Philippines, Encyclopedia Britannica (updated 2020), as cited in Wikipedia
2. Census of the Philippines, Encyclopedia Britannica (updated 2020), as cited in Wikiped

Pictures of the Polillo Group of Islands and Field Trips

From top left: CESO work group – Town of Polillo; CESO assignment SWOT session; Public engagement for CESO project – Polillo Island; Initial feast on Polillo Island; The boat on the Polillo Island field trip; Bato Beach WW2 structure; Pregnant woman's pageant; Seaweed Harvesting structure; Norelco diesel energy plant; Traveling on the road trail – Polillo to Burdeos; Edling rescuing me from the ledge by the cave near Burdeos; A feast – Burdeos island hopping field trip

Pictures of the Polillo Group of Islands and Field Trips

From top left: Solar panel on Edling's home; Pearl farm; Sweet smelling Ylang Ylang; Exiting the boat – offshore at Infanta; Lumber delivery by donkey; Hard labour at a cement plant; Man swimming with his horse; Boatman taking me to Panukulan; With Panukulan Mayor, Councilor and Administrator; Fully loaded tricycle and sidecar; Rural housing – Burdeos; Inoculation of a child in Panukulan

The Mighty Caribao and Pictures with Participants from CESO Assignments in Alabat and the Polillo Islands

From top left: Rice bag delivery – cart and Caribao; Caribao – staple of Philippine agriculture; Pristine coral reef; Stingless bee colony hosted by an anchor ball; Wonderful Filipino hosts and happy hour; CESO Exit meeting – Polillo Island assignment; Building construction with bamboo scaffolding; Mayor Mesa of Alabat and myself; CESO assignment photo opp Alabat Island; CESO assignment photo opp Town of Polillo; CESO assignment photo opp Burdeos; CESO assignment photo opp Panukulan

Chapter 5

THE PHILIPPINES

Assignments in the Northern Batanes Islands in 2017
and Bulacan State University in 2019

Map prepared by Lance Smith

About the Batanes Islands

The seven islands that make up the Batanes region are located in the northernmost province of the Philippines. Batanes is the smallest province in terms of both population and land area. Its capital is the town of Basco, located on the main island of Batan. The island group is located approximately 162 kilometers (101 miles) north of the Luzon mainland and about 190 kilometers (120 miles) south of Taiwan.[1] The total provincial population on all the islands is about 18,000 square kilometers.[2] Batanes has a distinct Ivatan culture, and the language and the landscape are truly unique, somewhat distinct from the rest of the Philippines.

After the flight from Canada departing on June 28, 2017, on the connecting Philippine Airlines, and with a layover at a Manila hotel, I was off to Basco, Batanes at five a.m. I was shuttled from the small airport at Basco to the hotel. I had an interesting first impression of the area. There were no trees. I had seen pictures of the Scottish Highlands, and to me this landscape looks similar. The reason for there being no trees was because of the frequency of typhoons and tropical storms in the middle of the ocean. In this open part of the North China Sea, any sizeable trees would simply topple in those high wind situations.

The CESO Assignment

As was the case for the CESO assignment on the Polillo Group of Islands, I had been selected as the first Canadian volunteer advisor to go to Batanes, another remote area. I was excited to take up this challenge. It was suggested to me that if the assignment was successful, it would be a "steppingstone" to other CESO projects in that area in the future. That is what happened, and other CESO advisors have since gone there.

The CESO assignment was about assisting Batanes in developing a branding and marketing program for tourism. Together with the provincial government's Department of Trade and Industry, the objective was to establish Batanes as a sought-after tourist destination while also ensuring that sustainable tourism practices preserved the province's heritage and culture. All the people involved with this assignment in Batanes were very committed, and they showed a remarkable amount of enthusiasm and support for the project. Intensive public engagement sessions were held, and a local artist developed a logo to comple-ment the newly adopted branding with an associated slogan, "Breathtaking Batanes—Explore Simplicity." Another successful CESO assignment!

The Introductory Tour of Batan Island

After settling in, the hosts then took Matt Navalta, the CESO country represen-tative for the Philippines, and his wife and I on a circle tour of the main island of Batan. The circular highway contained several radical jigs and jags along the rugged coastline. There were signs to warn you of the sharp corners, stating, "Blow UR Horn." This is also a popular slogan used on souvenir coffee mugs sold there. Throughout the Philippines, you find small convenience stores, referred to by Filipinos as "sary sary" stores. In Batanes, you have Honesty Stores. Coffee, staple foods, and snacks are sold in Honesty Stores, but there is nobody inside the store. You pay by the honour system, into a tin cup. I am told everyone always pays, and there is never any theft. That was remarkable.

I was amused to see three wind terminals lying flat on one of the larger hills, and they had all been blown down in a typhoon or storm several years ago. They were never repaired and put back into operation. That is too bad because cleaner power would be preferable to the diesel generators used as the source of electrical power throughout the seven islands. The replacement parts were too expensive, so the broken wind terminals were simply left on the ground.

Active Sports in Batanes

I have been to the Philippines a total of seven times, and I was quite surprised to see a baseball tournament taking place while I was in Basco. Where I grew up on the Canadian prairies, baseball is a popular summer sport and tournaments are commonplace. Basketball is the most popular sport in the Philippines, but this was the first time I ever saw baseball being played anywhere in that country. It was a sports weekend on Batan Island. A basketball tournament was also happening at the same time. That was an impressive sports day. I took some time to watch some of the baseball games, but it was so hot outside I did not last too long.

A Weekend on Sabtang Island

My wife Clarita, and children Riley, Dylan, and Danika joined me in Basco, midway through my time working on that assignment. They accompanied me on much of the stay at the Batanes Islands. We took the short boat ride to nearby Sabtang Island, the second most populated island, home to magnificent white sand beaches. This was a spectacular place. It was not a fancy or well-known tourism destination, not very commercialized, but it was a place I will never forget. There was Morong Beach, with a naturally formed rock archway referred to as "Ahaw," very warm water, and waves which rocked you gently as you wade into the water.

There was a zip line from the mountain that ended at Sabtang beach, and Clarita tried it. I would say it was a one-kilometer ride. She loved it. I "chickened-out" at the last minute. I have some regrets about not joining her, but the zip-line belt was too tight on my groin area - ouch, and that was my excuse for the record.

Fundacion Pacita

On the edge of the town of Basco on Batan Island was the Fundacion Pacita Batanes Nature Lodge and Art Gallery. This fabulous facility contains an art museum, art school and historical museum facility with many very high-quality artworks, murals, and artifacts on display. At the lodge there were cottages to rent for a cultural tourism experience. Protogenes Galarion was the resident art director, and he helped with the CESO marketing and branding assignment in the development of a branding logo and the result was excellent. This facility is a must see for anyone visiting the Basco and Batanes Islands.

The Ivatan Stone Houses

There were many stone houses throughout the Batanes Islands, a unique feature in the Philippines. Houses were made of stone and concrete, and the walls were very thick. The reason for this is the typhoons and extreme winds that occur during, what the locals refer to as, the "rainy season." Weaker structures made of less durable materials will be blown down; hence, most houses are constructed of concrete and stone, and then they do not get blown down.

Clarita and I were told by the locals that to have the authentic experience of the Ivatan culture, we needed to sleep overnight in a stone hut. Areas of Sabtang Island with the stone houses are designated as a UNESCO world heritage site. So, we stayed overnight and rented a stone house. It was ridiculously hot and like being in an oven all night long. This was supposed to be a thrilling event, but the family was not happy with me. It was almost impossible to sleep on thin bamboo mats on top of concrete. Claire and Riley went to sleep on the beach. Dylan, Danika, and I slept on those mats in the heat inside the stone house, and we barely survived the heat.

Before leaving Sabtang Island, we saw the crazy looking headgear called Vakul which is headgear of the Ivatan women, designed to protect them from wind and rain. They are made from plant materials. These are mostly just sold to tourists today. Following this Sabtang Island adventure and an island tour, our family took the boat back to Basco on the main island of Batan.

Itbayat Island

While in Batanes, I ventured to the island of Itbayat. My family did not join me on this trip, as they arrived a few days later. It was a challenge to get to that remote island as described in the earlier chapter, but there were interesting things to see, after overcoming the scary ocean voyage that was described in chapter three. Of interest was a lengthy hike to a cave, another experience with stalagmites and interesting rock formations. This cave was less risky to observe than the cave in Burdeos LGU, in Quezon Province, which I had visited a few years earlier. Thank goodness for that! It was a long hike to get to those caves but seeing them was worth it. Noteworthy on Itbayat Island were the extremely sharp, steep cliffs. I did not want to get too close to the edge, as it was a long, long way down to the ocean, but they sure did offer beautiful views.

A Reward for Hard Work

The challenging work during the CESO assignment was rewarded with a fine meal of local favourite, coconut crab. It was very tasty. After the meal, there was an evening of karaoke. I think my attempt at singing may have caused some ear damage to those in the room. That work assignment seemed to be quite successful, and it was well received by the host. I enjoyed the adventures in the Batanes Islands as well. Despite the challenges of sleeping in stone houses, my family and I did enjoy the visit very much.

Bulacan State University—2019

Bulacan State University (BulSU) is located about a one-hour drive north of Manila, depending on traffic, and you can expect time delays when travelling through the city. I was informed that the campus has a student population of about 45,000. CESO had undertaken several projects at BulSU, and other CESO advisors had visited there before me, but this was my first time to go that university within the city of Malolos.

The Bulacan CESO Assignment

I was selected in the summer of 2019, to undertake a CESO assignment for the development of an energy management system (EMS) at the university. The campus wanted to save money, reduce the amount of energy wasted, and the amount of GHG greenhouse gases generated by the campus – in response to the challenge that climate change poses on planet earth. My previous experience in Canada, and particularly as a city planner in Peachland, BC, included the development of an energy management system in that city, as part of climate change action planning work being done under my direction. I felt comfortable doing a similar project at BulSU and directing the EMS management and training. The technical data collection and the calculations were done by the BulSU engineers. I made a few Skype calls to my engineer friend in Canada, Mike Seibert, and he provided technical energy management expertise for engineers at BulSU. He was a significant help. My input was in program management and in the implementation of the system, so with Mike's assistance, the technical aspects for this assignment were also covered as well. This project went remarkably well and met the expectations of the client at BulSU.

Working Together and Coordinating Action

I had become quite familiar with governance issues and challenges in the Philippines. In my career in Canada, my work usually encompassed collaboration, consultation, and networking. This was how to get commitment and "buy-in" from the client for progressive action and change. These were key elements of Canadian governance technology which could be transferred to the client. This approach was shared in the Philippines, and it assisted the governance there. The campus staff seemed very receptive to the help provided.

At BulSU, inputs and consultations on the project involved different internal faculties. Campus energy consumption was mostly from electrical energy generation (lighting and air conditioning) and transportation—for their vehicle fleet use and maintenance and the office equipment. The project involved connecting with external agencies involved with energy issues. That included MERALCO (the Energy utility provider in Bulacan) and the city of Molalos. The Procurement Division and central budgeting agency under the President's Office at BulSU were also part of the process. This coordination was important to place higher priority on green purchases for energy efficient vehicles, equipment, and supplies. This project also involved the BulSU Communications Department. They needed to establish messaging throughout the university to promote responsible energy conservation behaviour by the students, university staff, as well as contractors that provided services to the university. After a few weeks of work, the client seemed pleased with the assistance provided, and I felt this Bulacan assignment was a successful one.

Batanes and from Bulacan State University through the Rear View Mirror

My assignments in Batanes and at the university in Bulacan were quite different, but both were interesting. Specific skills were necessary to conduct these projects, but most important was the need to foster teamwork and get the various stakeholders together, to collaborate and find solutions and actions necessary to address their challenges. The final reports for both assignments hit the mark. I continued with other assignments visiting the Philippines up until 2019. My high regard for the Philippines has remained intact – these assignments and the other adventures encountered were fantastic. The more times I visit and explore the Philippines, the more I want to return to that wonderful country.

FOOTNOTES

1. Philatlas – Atlas of the Philippines (2015); as cited in Wikipedia;
2. Census of the Philippines, Philippine Statistics Authority Encyclopedia Britannica (2020); cited in Wikipedia

Travels and CESO Assignments in the Batanes Islands and at Bulacan State University

From top left: Meeting with the Batanes Governor and Officials – 2017; CESO work sessions in Batanes – 2017; CESO assignment photo opp; Vacul hats – Ivatan culture of Philippines; A stone house in Batanes; The Ahaw rock formation; Sharp curves – Blow UR horn sign; Damaged wind terminal; Field trip on Itbuyet Island in Batanes; CESO Bulacan assignment work session; CESO Energy Management Assignment – 2019 in Bulacan State University; CESO BulSU assignment Photo Opp

Chapter 6

THE PHILIPPINES

Exploring Parts of the Visayas Region and the Palawan Islands:
2012 – 2017

SOUTH
CHINA
SEA

PHILIPPINES

• MANILA

PHILLIPINE
SEA

CEBU

BOHOL

PALAWAN

Map prepared by Lance Smith

Background on the Visayas Region

The Visayas region or the Visayan Islands, is one of the three main geographical divisions of the Philippines, along with Luzon and Mindanao. The area contains a population of almost twenty million people, located in the central part of the Philippines. This division consists of several islands, primarily surrounding the Visayan Sea, although the Visayas are also considered the northeast extremity of the entire Sulu Sea. Its inhabitants are the Visayan peoples. The Visayas region is not only identified for geographical reasons, but one will notice that there are distinct characteristics, customs, and languages in areas throughout this region. [1]

After completion of this CESO assignments, my family joined me for extended vacations. We toured the Visayas and Palawan regions, and we saw interesting places. These travels were new and different experiences from those enjoyed in other parts of the Philippines. The Visayas and Palawan regions were referred to as "must see" places and they did not disappoint.

Boracay

Boracay, one of the most popular islands for tourists in the Philippines, is highly rated worldwide. Boracay is a small island, seven kilometers long and one kilometer wide, located in the western part of the Visayas region. It is approximately 315 kilometers south of Manila and two kilometers off the northwest tip of Panay Island. Boracay had a population of 32,267 as of February 2016. [2]

Because of the reputation of this destination, our family decided to go there in 2012, just before Christmas. We took this trip after the CESO work assignment in Lucban. It was fortunate that we were able to go there before 2018 because at that time, the island and all its resorts were closed for about a year. [3] The closure was because of environmental conditions, specifically the disposal of sanitary sewer wastes into the ocean without treatment. At that time the infrastructure and sewage treatment were upgraded to a higher standard and the resort areas of Boracay opened again in 2019, and they are now flourishing.

For our family, getting to Boracay during 2012 was indeed very tricky. After leaving Manila airport, which was an adventure, we landed at the airport in the town of Caticlan. This airport serves the Boracay resort. We then took tricycle taxis (two of them for six people) to a port and then we took a ten-minute ferry ride on a small-sized boat to Boracay Island. After departing from the airport, there was another twenty-minute tricycle taxi ride, this time to our accommodations which were further up the island. It was in the area called Station 2—the family section. You could say the transportation transitioning from air to water to land was another Indiana Jones experience. That shuttle experience was crazy. We had to compete for tricycle taxis and wait in line-ups for the shuttle ferry. My wife had packed far too much luggage, and it was painful when loading the luggage onto smaller boats and the taxis. I also made a huge mistake. At each transfer point, there was porter assistance, and I paid a tip. I got mixed up over the value of the money exchange (Canadian dollar vs. Philippine peso) and after finally reaching the destination to the hotel, I realized I had given over $100 in tips. I was not very smart that day.

We had five nice days of enjoying the gorgeous white sand beach in Boracay, swimming and snorkeling, and especially a nice catered meal set up for us on the beach. One evening, we watched a group of Chinese tourists enjoying a floating lantern ceremony. We were told this was a symbol of hope for the future. It was impressive to see this after dark, as all these lighted lanterns floated into the sky and eventually burned up and disintegrated.

Bohol

We visited other places in the Visayas region during visits to the Philippines. In 2014, we travelled to Cebu and Bohol. Clarita wanted to go there, but I was not sure because it was a long distance from the main island of Luzon where we were always based. But Clarita's wishes prevailed, and it was a good thing they did. There were many interesting things to see in Bohol and in Cebu.

Bohol Island is also located in the Visayas region, and we were told it had a population of about 21,000. This island had things you would never see elsewhere. There was a snake sanctuary with taxidermy displaying several species including one of the biggest python snakes ever discovered.

We visited the chocolate hills—strange natural landscape of hills. These hills were naturally formed from weathered limestone over thousands of years, but it looked as if they were manicured to create perfect hill landscapes. In the dry season time of year, they are brown, hence why they are called the chocolate hills. We were told of legends suggesting the hills were created from giants fighting each other and disrupting the terrain. Not so believable, but such myths make this an entertaining story.

We also took a boat tour out into the ocean, saw a dolphin-run where dolphins were jumping in the air. We also enjoyed some snorkeling and in front of us our guide shelled some live sea urchins. We ate these urchins directly out of their shells during our time snorkeling. They tasted incredibly good. This all occurred near a large, shallow reef, and we were actually about two kilometres from shore. It seemed like we were in the middle of the Pacific Ocean.

Finally, there was a park containing a rare, endangered species - the Tarsier. These are being protected at the Tarsier Conservation Area. They are tiny creatures—like miniature meerkats but very fragile, and they need to be protected. It was a special privilege to see them.

Cebu

Our family only spent two short days in Cebu, the second biggest city in the Philippines (Manila- 20 million; Cebu- 3 million people). There were some interesting things to see, and in our short stay. We saw a museum which provided information and some fabulous monuments in tribute to Lapu Lapu and the Filipino warriors, who defeated the Spanish in 1521. Despite the heroic actions of Filipino heroes, the interpretive display indicated that this did not stop 300 years of colonization by the Spaniards.

We also saw the Chinese Taoist Temple overlooking the Cebu, which was like transplanting a piece of China into the Philippines. It was beautiful architecture to see. There was much more to see in Cebu, but the city was not on our schedule of places where we were going to spend much time.

The Palawan Island Region

The Palawan Island region is the western-most province in the Philippines and is within the South China Sea. The province contained about 1,105,000 people in 2017. [4] It is a highly regarded tourist destination with beautiful beaches and landscapes and rich biodiversity like many other areas in the Philippines. We were told it is the only part of the Philippines that has never experienced an earthquake or volcanic eruption.

Puerto-Princessa and Paddling through the Underground River in Southern Palawan

After the CESO assignment in Batanes, and after spending some time there, my family travelled together to the Palawan islands. Clarita's brother June, from the Philippines, again accompanied us - our highly valued driver, guide, and protector.

Our first stop in Palawan was near the region's largest city, Puerta Princessa. We stayed at a resort near the Subterranean River National Park, a UNESCO protected biosphere reserve. This famous cave contains a river, and you paddle into the cave in a boat on the river. It is just over eight kilometers in length, the longest underground river in a cave in the world. This cave contains stalactites and stalagmite icicles, which we were told, were environmentally fragile and should not be touched. This was enforced by officers at the destination. Only one and a half kilometers of the river was open for viewing by boat. This was a magnificent tour experience. However, there were more bats flying around in this cave than I could ever have imagined – millions if anyone counted them.

As we paddled through the cave, I was in the first seat. The bats suddenly flew at us and one of the bats flew close to me and the wing touched my ear. Not expecting this, a frightening experience. I was grateful that it was me in the front seat of the boat and not any of the others. I was fine and there was no harm resulting, but the episode was something out of a horror movie. The rest of the paddling experience was relaxing, although very dark and with dim lighting. We were restricted from taking any pictures, so this experience can only be described in words, not pictures.

Animals Outside the Cave

Outside the cave tunnel and a short distance away along the shore, there were a few young monitor lizards. These reptiles are dangerous, and all visitors were required to keep a safe distance away from them. There were also a lot of monkeys in the trees. All ladies were asked to hang on tightly to their purses since these monkeys were not intimidated by humans and were known to snatch any unprotected purses. We departed from the cave area, and as we continued our way to our hotel, we noticed the karst limestone rock formations along the shore, and these were stunning landscapes.

El Nido–the Middle of Palawan Region

Moving further north on the island of Palawan, we also visited El Nido. We rented a van at the resort near Puerta Princessa to take us on the five-to six-hour drive. I recall buying cashew nuts and rambutan fruit from a stand at the side of the road. The area has a reputation for growing the highest quality cashews in the world. Rambutan is an unusual looking tropical fruit, reddish in colour, with what looks like spears surrounding. It is difficult to peel, but the fruit tasted quite good.

El Nido is a popular tourism area. It contains a wide variety of restaurants, bars, massage parlours, and souvenir shops. Many people who go there are more interested in island hopping and spending relaxing time at resort hotels on some of the other islands. We did that and it was nice, although quite expensive. While island hopping near one of the small islands near to the Minilock resort, referred to in chapter three - this is where our family, encountered a severe tropical storm. That was a day of vacation pleasure mixed with a scary adventure.

The Resort Near El Nido – Not Always Impressed

There was an incident which was quite disappointing to me. While staying at Minilock, the food, accommodations, and scenery were outstanding. However, every afternoon at about two o'clock, everyone was told to leave the beach area. The resort began pumping all its liquid waste including huge volumes of soap-suds and dishwashing water, into the beach area. The resort avoided the time and expense of treating the wastewater and instead flushed it into the beach area, mixing with the ocean water. Eventually, it would wash away, "out of sight, out of mind." After about two hours, the beach was fine. No more soap suds. This was a disappointing environmental practice. I am not a technical expert on this, but I know that was polluting the ocean. I was so extremely disappointed in that reputable, high-price resort. Although I expressed concerns to the resort owner, I do not think my concern was taken too seriously.

Travelling to Caron—the Northern Part of Palawan

After two days in El Nido, our family departed on the Montenegro fast ferry, which took about three and a half hours to get to Caron, in the northern Palawan Islands. This area contains some of the best opportunities for tourism diving in the world, with underwater shipwrecks to explore. Not being divers, our family did not do this.

Near to Caron, we stayed at another attractive resort, the Two Seasons. We relaxed, did some kayaking, swimming on the beach, and visited a therapeutic hot spring. Not too much of an Indiana Jones adventure here, but it was genuinely nice, although it rained almost the whole time during the few days that we stayed there.

At the Maquinat hot spring near Caron, I met a retired American cattle rancher from Montana, USA. This state is near the Canadian border. The rancher had been recruited to come to Palawan several years earlier. He was a rancher and an expert in the field of cattle breeding. He told me that there had been a limited diversification of livestock breeding opportunity - so the cattle gene pool needed to be enhanced in Palawan. Over time was a declining quality of the meat being produced and a high rate of disease in the cattle in Palawan. This guy was recruited by the Philippine government to improve the cattle reproduction practices and he had imported North American cattle to Palawan. He told us that the result of these efforts over the past decade had been the development of healthier, higher quality cattle throughout Palawan. This gentleman now has a second home there, and he married to a Filipino woman from Palawan . . . an interesting story.

The Visayas and Palawan Regions in the Rear View Mirror

There are so many things to see in the Philippines. The Visayas area is different from other areas of the country - lots of coconut trees, white sand beaches, and many small inlands. There is good access to the ocean, and the Visayas region offers a slightly different culture and different languages (not just Tagalog), as well as unique food, climate, and geography.

Palawan is also a tropical paradise, even more frequented by tourists these days, and people say it has replaced Boracay as the number one tourist destination in the Philippines. Palawan is a beautiful area for relaxation, and there are many pleasurable things to do there.

After each trip to the Philippines, I realized that no matter where I went, there was always something special to see, moments of adventure, opportunities to meet new friends, see unfamiliar places, and expose yourself to new and different foods. This country is truly amazing.

FOOTNOTES

1. Census of the Philippines (2015)
2. Census of the Philippines (2015)
3. Boy Ryan Zobal, Pinay News, (April 19, 2019) – article cited in Wikipedia
4. Census of the Philippines (2015)
5. Census of the Philippines (2015)

Pictures From Travels to the Visayas and Palawan Island Regions

From top left: Arrival by boat at Boracay 2012; Snorkeling at Boracay; Danika at the Boracay lookout; Boys eating on Boracay beach; The Chocolate Hills in Bohol; Tarsier Conservation Area in Bohol; The Swinging Bridge – Bohol; A world record python snake, Bohol; Minilock Resort Beach near El Nido, Palawan; Paddling into the Underground River, Palawan; monitor lizard – Palawan; Statues of Lapu Lapu, Philippine hero, Cebu

Chapter 7

THE PHILIPPINES

Exploring Areas in Northern Luzon: 2012-2017

Map prepared by Lance Smith

Tarlac

After completing CESO assignments in the Philippines, when accompanied by my wife, we always went to visit her family. Although living in Canada since 1989, Clarita hails from the City of Tarlac, north of Manila. I was able experience and enjoy the Filipino culture in a rather intimate way, at the family level, through family events held in Tarlac.

Tarlac is two and a half hours north of Manila, located inland, and not on the coast. It contains a population of about 1.5 million, and the capital, Tarlac City, contains about a half million people. [1] The area is largely agriculturally based, growing primarily rice and sugar cane. This is also the home of recent president Binigno Aquino and his mother Cory, who was a former president. In the 1970s, Binigno's father was a politician opposing the president at that time. Ninoy was assassinated during the reign of then President Ferdinand Marcos. This well-known tragic event, and it is connected to Tarlac's history, because it is the homeland of the Aquino family. Our family visited the Aquino Center Museum in Tarlac in 2014 and we viewed interpretive details and displays which told the story of those events.

A Filipino Wedding and a Baby Christening

While in Tarlac in 2014, our family attended the wedding of Clarita's niece Joy. She is the daughter of Alfredo and Julieta Aguinaldo who immigrated to Kelowna, Canada along with their other three children (Kevin, Mary Joyce and Kristine) in 2007. That wedding was a magnificent day. Our family was on the list of wedding sponsors, as family, and VIP donators for the event. I was also asked to give a speech toasting the bride, and I did that. It was wonderful to be there and to play a prominent part in such an important event.

We were also invited to attend a christening event for one of Clarita's nephews to celebrate his recently born child. Christenings are an important celebration for Filipinos. Following the ceremony there was a feast of *lechon* (roast pig), *caldereta* (goat), and vegetables. I think about a hundred people attended that event, held outdoors in a large, covered tent structure. Such a festivity for a christening is not usually celebrated to that extent in Canada.

Staying at a Midwife Birthing Facility

While in Tarlac in 2017, our family stayed at a midwife birthing facility, which was owned and run by Vangie Aguinaldo, the sister-in-law of my wife Clarita. She is not a doctor, but she is a qualified midwife. Midwives are the primary agents for the delivery of babies in the Philippines. They work in facilities outside of hospitals. This is a cost effective and safe system, an alternative to hospital birthing, which is the North American system. We were able to stay there because there were extra comfortable rooms at the birthing centre during the time that we were there. The centre had air-conditioning, so this turned out to be good accommodations for us. However, there were some noisy moments during the night when young mothers came into the facility to give birth, sometimes in rushed circumstances. I was not expecting to stay in a place like this, but it turned out to be fine for us.

Lechon for Special Occasions and Respect for Older People

Filipino people love to eat roast pork—lechon, and for most special occasions, which is the prize dish served. It requires slow cooking a pig on a stick over a fire, and it is done with special care and attention. I had the opportunity to be involved in that process.

Respect is important in the Filipino culture. An example is pagmamano, where younger people bow their head before older people and place their forehead on the back of the hand of the older person. This strikes me as a very touching gesture of respect. I was regularly the recipient of the pagmamano process, and this was very gratifying and meaningful once you understand the cultural significance. It seems to me that respect and gratitude are a disappearing aspect of North American life in recent years. That is not the case in the Philippines.

A Visit to a Rural School

In the Pata Pata area just outside of Tarlac City, we visited an elementary and middle school in 2017. While there for only a short time, the teachers gave us a surprise. In very short order, they organized a band concert with the students' playing instruments and marching. The young students were quite talented, and this was a special honour bestowed upon our family.

Mount Pinatobo—Now a Dormant Volcano

In 2012, our family, along with members of Clarita's family in the Philippines, went on a hike to Mount Pinatubo, located forty-five kilometres from Tarlac City and about ninety kilometers from Manila, which would be a three-hour drive. Major volcanic eruptions at Mount Pinatubo occurred from June until August 1991, killing a total of 722 people, and leaving over 100,000 people homeless. This event may have been the largest volcanic eruption of the twentieth century. [2]

This crater was difficult to get to. First, convoys of jeep vehicles drove tourists for several kilometre to the start-point for a long hike on foot. Then it was a seven- kilometre hike to the Crater Lake. A very, very tiring day it was, travelling with our family of smaller children at the time. But this volcano was a special site, and that hike would have been a challenge for Indiana Jones as well. It was such an enjoyable experience visiting a place of such historic significance in the Philippines.

Bagio City

Bagio City is a fascinating place to visit. We visited Bagio City, a five-hour drive north of Manila, on three occasions between 2012 and 2017. It is within the central Cordillera mountains area of northern Luzon, and at higher elevations, has a cooler climate, at least by Filipino standards. It is the largest city in the region, with about 350,000 people. [3] It is often referred to as the summer capital of the country. It receives a lot of tourists, and I would say it is the hub of northern Luzon.

Good City Planning

Being a city planner, I am familiar with Daniel Burham, a force in early planning and influenced by the "city beautiful movement," [4] which was an attempt to make cities more attractive and livable during the early 1900s. The significance of this movement was incorporating prominent public architecture and significant parks into cities. Burnham took a leading role in the creation of master plans for city development—Baguio and Manila in the Philippines, and also in master plans completed for Chicago, Cleveland, San Francisco and downtown Washington, D.C., in the USA.[5]

Baquio City is a city almost surrounded by mountains and at the floor of this valley at the center of the city, is this large Burham Park. The tourist information indicated the park is 82 acres (32.8 hectares) in size. Wherever you are in Baguio, all eyes tend to focus on beautiful Burham Park, particularly the surrounding mountain slopes where most of the residents live. It is like being in a stadium and watching a sporting event, except the park is the central attraction. What great city planning. Another feature is the streets of Baguio. These are not like the linear, traditional grid pattern of roadways. Instead, they follow the contours of the terrain, more in harmony with the natural landscape and this is much more interesting.

An Uninvited Guest for Dinner

During our most recent visit to Baguio City in 2017, our family stopped at a covered, open-air restaurant to eat. The food looked sensational. We sat down and started to eat the wonderful seafood, *pancit (*noodles), *lumpia* (spring rolls), *adobo* (a spicy Filipino meat dish), and some other foods. It was no surprise that it started to rain (it was the rainy season), and no sooner was the food being served, when a large rat scurried across the floor to escape the heavy rain. It ran past me, only a few inches from my feet, and then scurried to the back of the restaurant. Despite the excellent food, we left that restaurant quickly. That was indeed a disturbing moment.

Despite heavy drenching rain, after leaving the restaurant we went shopping at the night market, which is what you do in Baguio City. It was open on Friday nights, from eight p.m. until midnight, I believe. We bought some interesting things that night. I enjoyed being able to bargain with the vendors and try to get a good deal. However, even with umbrellas, we were all wet by the time we returned to the hotel. It was certainly a different kind of shopping experience.

Banaue–North of Baguio City

In 2014, our family travelled to Banaue, about a six-hour drive north of Bagio City. The local municipality contains about 22,000 people [6], most scattered throughout the rural areas, with perhaps a few thousand people in the town. The Banaue Rice Terraces were carved into the mountains of Banaue by the ancestors of the Indigenous Ifugao people. The terraces are referred to as the "Eighth Wonder of the World". [7] The terraces were built by hard manual labour, by hand, and without mechanical equipment. An amazing feat! The day we were there it was rainy and foggy, so the weather was not ideal for viewing those terraces, but we saw them. This area is a popular tourist attraction and there are some fabulous craft shops in the town as well.

One Hundred Islands

One Hundred Islands is a popular tourist destination and an interesting, beautiful but unusual area to see. The Hundred Islands National Park was the first national park designated a protected area in the Philippines. It is adjacent to Alaminos (population 82,000), within Pangasinan Province (population just under 3 million) in this part of the northern Philippines. [8] The actual number of islands varies depending on the tide, as some get submerged at high tide. It is safe to say that there are greater than one hundred islands located off the coast of Alaminos at Lingayen Gulf. The area is located a couple of hours from Tarlac City in northern Luzon, en-route to Baguio City. The tourist information indicated these islands cover an area of just under seventeen square kilometers (6.5 square miles).

While touring the One Hundred Islands and island hopping on the small boats, zigzagging between them, we stopped for lunch and swimming. One of those islands had been totally taken over by bats. There were many more bats than there were trees on that island. That was something I had never seen before. We experienced a similar experience on our family side trip to the Subterranean River National Park near Porta Princessa, Palawan in 2017.

My son Riley, nine years old at the time, discovered jellyfish, and he looked at and played with giant clam taklobo shells on the shore. These were very impressive. They seemed to be more fun for him than Lego blocks.

"The NHL (National Hockey League) Playoffs

Although nobody in the Philippines was interested in hockey, I am a Canadian who loves hockey. My history of once playing junior league hockey, coaching kids, playing for many years in adult "beer leagues" and always following the NHL playoffs has something to do with that. While in Canada, there are usually playoff games on the television every night during April, May and into June. In 2014, my CESO assignment and the travel while there was during the month of May. It was difficult to keep current with the daily hockey scores. Through an internet search at the hotel a day earlier, I was aware that the Chicago Black Hawks (my favourite team), were tied 3-3 in a seven game semi-final series with the Los Angeles Kings. The day of that important game, after my CESO assignment, my family and I were travelling from Tarlac to One Hundred Islands. The van we were travelling in got a flat tire. We were delayed a long time until that tire was taken to the nearest town, to be repaired. It just so happened that the flat tire occurred in front of a roadside internet café. During the delay I entered the café and rented a computer stall. I wanted to determine the status of that game. As it turned out, the game was in progress, tied 4-4 and was going into overtime. Through a website search, I was able to follow a ticker-tape play-by-play description of that overtime as the game progressed into two overtime sessions. Unfortunately, Chicago lost in the overtime, but what a strange twist of fate that was - to follow that important hockey game in live time, in the Philippines.

The Beaches of Bolinao

From Alaminos, three hours north of Tarlac City, you can drive directly north for about an hour to Bolinao. Many attractive resorts are in that area, and our family stayed at a beautiful place—Puerto de Sol. Clarita and I were able to get a "Hilot massage," a Filipino-style deep tissue therapeutic massage at the resort, and it was fantastic.

We traveled around that resort region near Bolinao and found an attraction called the Enchanted Cave. There was a swimming area quite far underground, ten or fifteen meters down some step stairs. We had a nice swim there, and the water was warm. Afterward, we found a lady selling some decorative handmade seashell wall hangs. They were so beautiful, we bought ten of them. It was a good day for the seller. There was also a small shop selling tobacco - giant dried leaves, which I was told were crushed, and then wrapped in cigarette paper. I am not a smoker, but I found this interesting to notice that tabaco was not purchased in packages.

The Northern Philippines in the Rear View Mirrow

The northern Luzon area contains a wide variety of things to see. My family and I did not see all of this region, but we were able to enjoy many activities, see interesting places, and gain further insight into life in this part of the Philippines. As I am connected to a Filipino family through marriage, this experience allowed me to get close, intimate insight into the culture and the celebrations they dearly love—the special occasions involving Clarita's family were particularly meaningful. I know how the people live, and I was able to experience their way of life. What a fun time!

FOOTNOTES

1. Census of the Philippines (2015)
2. US Geological Survey publication (recent update May 16, 2018)
3. Census of the Philippines (2015)
4. Naomi Blumberg, Assistant Editor, Arts and Culture for Encyclopedia Britannica (2015) article cited in Wikipedia
5. McBrien, Judith Payne, Daniel Burham: Life and Work; Encyclopedia Britannica(2015)article cited in Wikipedia
6. Census of the Philippines (2015)
7. The Best' of the Philippines - its natural wonders, Filipinasoul.com (May 11, 2014) article cited in Wikipedia
8. Census of the Philippines (2015)

Pictures of Travels Through Northern Luzon

From top left: Our Niece's wedding in the Philippines; My Toast to the bride; Clarita's family in Tarlac, Philippines – 2017; Baby christening; The midwife birthing center; Roasting a pig – Lechon; Pagmamano – Philippine tradition of respect; Visiting a school near Tarlac; Hiking to Mount Pinatubo; Crater Lake on top of Mount Pinatubo; Burnham Park in Baquio City; Baquio night market – open in the rain

Pictures of Travels Through Northern Luzon

From top left: A rat came to dinner – Baquio City; Rice Terraces in Banuae; Ifugao – the indigenous culture in Banaue; Nice souvenirs in Banaue; Island hopping at 100 Islands; Clarita and I at the 100 Island lookout; Son Riley with a jellyfish; Proliferation of bats in a tree – 100 Islands; Swimming in the Enchanted Cave – Bolinao; A Filipino hilot massage at Bolinao; Sea shell shades and lamps – roadside purchases; Tobacco leaves for sale

Chapter 8

THE PHILIPPINES

Finding a Way to Help the Philippines While in Canada: Solar Electricity for Remote Schools in the Polillo Group of Islands

*Picture provided courtesy of the Infanta Rotary Club, Philippines, 2017

Planning and Fund-raising for a Solar Electricity Project

The Philippines is special to me. Since 2012, I have ventured there seven times, and completed thirteen assignments for CESO. I travelled throughout Luzon in the northern part of the country, to the Visayas region in the middle, and to Palawan Island. I always love to return to the Philippines and see areas I have not seen before. With over 7000 islands, there are always new places to discover.

Many people struggle to survive in the Philippines. After each visit, when I have returned to Canada, I have a strong passion to do good things for these people. In addition to the numerous assignments and well-intended non-profit volunteer work I have completed in the Philippines, I decided to embark on a personal project. In 2015, while staying at a lodge in Burdeos,

Polillo Island, something happened which really moved me. A lady school-teacher and her colleagues who were staying at the Albert lodge in Burdeos, told me a story about their teaching at schools in outlying, remote areas. In some of those regions, there was no electric power available at all and this made teaching challenging for them. The electrical power was rationed in the settled regions of Polillo Island - that was bad enough. But people in the rural, less populated areas and on the smaller isolated islands adjacent to Polillo Island faced an even greater burden, living their daily lives without any electrical power at all.

Madobel Morada was a teacher of small stature, about 4'10" in size, but she had a huge passion for teaching children. She taught in an extremely remote area in Bonifasio Barangay, within Burdeos municipality. She told me, with tears in her eyes, that it was extremely hard to instruct children, especially during days when it was not sunny. She said she always prayed for an electricity solution so that the students could have on-going light in the classroom, use computers and visual aids. She also told me many children walked several kilometers to school, and some made the journey by boat. Many times, they would come to school very wet due to the rain, and they were often hungry because they did not have enough to eat. This was a sad story.

When I returned to Canada after the CESO assignment in 2015, I could not get this conversation out of my mind. While in Burdeos, I had worked with Edling Tallisayon, Municipal Director of Planning and Development. I knew that Edling had installed a small solar power system at his residence in Burdeos because I had seen it when I visited his family. I contacted Edling via email (sometimes relayed through Matt Navalta the CESO CR in the Philippines) and asked him if similar solar panels could be installed at remote schools. He indicated that they could. Following our communication, he did some work to find the solar panel supplies and other costs involved for such a project. These were provided to me and the Rotary Club in Canada.

My next step, after receiving the solar design and cost estimates, was to seek funding for such an undertaking. CESO is a volunteer organization that engages with local partners to deliver sustainable development results in response to local needs. The assignment on Polillo Island was completed in 2015. It was necessary to find a funding sponsor for this specific project. I knew a few people who belong to Rotary Club's in Canada—a service club with a mandate is to fund meaningful international projects around the world. Upon my return to Canada, I made presentations to members at a couple of clubs in the Okanagan Valley to see if special project funding could be found. To my surprise, late in 2017, the solar project funding was granted through the Peachland Rotary Club – in the Municipality where I had previously worked. This club was able to make a connection with another Rotary Club in Infanta, Philippines. Infanta is on the coast of Luzon, facing Polillo Island. It is located about four and a half hours travelling time from Burdeos (three hours by boat, ninety minutes by land). This successful connection was established.

I was in regular contact with Wolfgang Muhs of the Peachland Rotary Club in Canada. Through his persistence and extraordinary efforts, as well as support from his colleagues including Chris Scowen, this solar panel project was successful. It was a unique project, and there were many "hoops to go through" to get it completed, but Wolfgang was persistent at every turn. In February 2018, six solar panels were installed at six schools in the remote area of Burdeos LGU, in the Polillo Group of Islands. These remote schools were in rural Baraguay areas within the LGU being Calutcut, Palasan, Bonifacio, Rizal, Carlagan, and Cabungalunan.

Sometimes Good Things Happen

I feel a true sense of satisfaction having contributed to doing a very positive project in the Philippines. I met wonderful, dedicated people who were focused and determined to make this solar energy project happen. It was a great pleasure to know that it was completed. The quality of teaching and the education of children in those remote areas, has been improved because of those solar panels. I have received communications from both from teachers in Burdeos and the sponsoring Rotary Clubs both in Canada and in Infanta in the Philippines expressing thanks for the initiation of this project.

One of my most lasting memories of time spent in the Philippines is the warmth of the people. Everywhere I went, people wanted to have a picture taken with this Caucasian visitor. The school children especially, always wanted a photo. Not so many foreigners ever travel the rural areas where I travelled. I was constantly involved with the taking of pictures while in that country - it is easy to smile in the Philippines.

Working with CESO has been one of the greatest joys of my life, and that was particularly true when working in the Philippines. These assignments allowed me to do positive work in the areas of poverty reduction and in transferring Canadian technology abroad. Connecting directly with the local people allowed me to have an authentic experience, to see the country, and have an intimate, lasting friendship with many of the people I met.

The solar project involved many well-meaning people who put a lot of effort into helping this get to the finish line. It took coordination between organizations both in Canada and in the Philippines. Rural, remote areas of the Philippines often get forgotten, from what I could see. I discovered how the education of children in these areas has been challenging. This project did not receive any funding from government, but it was a remarkable success.

It was a blessing for me to go to the Philippines and see so much of the beautiful country, as well as to be able to contribute in a small way to improving the conditions there.

Pictures of the Solar Panel Project in the Philippines

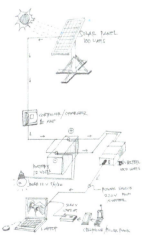

From top left: Madobel Morada – Burdeos teacher asked for help; Edling Tallisayon – helped with a plan; First solar panel installed in 2017; Infanta Rotary Club with schoolteachers – 2017; Trail to Bonifacio School; Some children take a boat to get to school; Meeting with a Philippine Rotary Club 2015; Children with benefit; A Certificate of Appreciation; The solar panel design plan; A Filipino dinner celebration >Pictures of the installed solar panel were provided by the Infanta Rotary Club. The pictures showing the Solar design and the cost estimates were provided by Edling Tallisayon, Coordinator of Planning and Development, Burdeos LGU.

Chapter 9

COLOMBIA

*The Coffee Triangle Assignments and Exploring
Parts of Colombia: 2016-2019*

Map produced by Lance Smith

About Colombia

From years of media reports and general hearsay, I thought Colombia was a dangerous country. However, during the four times I was there between 2016 and 2019, I found Colombia to be comfortable and safe, particularly in the province of Quindio and the coffee triangle where I spent most of my time.

That said, Colombia was at the epicenter of the Western Hemisphere's drug wars from 1958-2013. Some 220,000 people died in the conflict (including 45,000 children). Five million people were displaced from their homes and 16 percent of Colombians engaged in the war between 1985 and 2010. [1] In my trips to Colombia, I had no violent encounters or exposure to any drug incidents at all. There was an observable presence of police and diligent security at the airports including dog-sniffing, in addition to the regular screening of luggage taking place at airports.

Pijao, located in Quindio Departmento (Province) is a small community of about 6,000 people. The town of Pijao is where I was staying most of the time during my visits to Colombia. As of 2010, Pijao and seven Departmentos were designated by the United Nations as a Coffee Cultural Landscape of Colombia, a designation of considerable status. Colombia is the third most populated country in Latin America, behind Brazil and Mexico. The land area of Colombia is 1.139 million square kilometers, slightly larger than the size of British Columbia, Canada, which is 944,735 square kilometers. Pijao is a small town located about fifty-five kilometers from the provincial capital of Armenia. Colombia is a very mountainous country, and Pijao is in the Andes Mountain range being at 1766 meters above sea level. [2] Colombia is really very special. It has endured a lot of tough times, and it is difficult to explain, but this country grabs hold of you, and it is a good feeling. It is because of the landscape and the people in Colombia, both of which are truly magnificent.

Travelling to Pijao, Colombia

My first CESO trip to Colombia for an assignment was in January 2016. My oldest son Lance came with me. Magdalen, his daughter, and my granddaughter, stayed at home for school, and I know it was hard for him to leave her behind. She is a sweetheart.

It was a long flight to Colombia. I left from the Kelowna airport in BC, and Lance left from Nanaimo, and we met in Vancouver the evening of January 28, 2016. We then took the *red eye*, an all-night Air Canada flight from Vancouver to Toronto, then a direct morning flight on January 29 from Toronto to Bogota, Colombia. There was a final connecting flight on Avianca Airlines from Bogota to Armenia, arriving in the evening. With all the connecting times involved, we arrived in Pijao late that evening, very tired. Lance and I were picked up at the airport in Armenia, where we were driven by car for another hour and twenty minutes to Pijao. That was an exhausting trip.

Fundacion Pijao Cittaslow

Our host was Monica Florez, coordinator for Fundacion Pijao Cittaslow, a non-governmental organization (NGO), who for many years has been attempting to do good things in her community. I would classify her as a dedicated and well-meaning activist. Her mission includes sustainable community development, engagement and participation, climate change actions, organic farming, and the promotion of an organic, green lifestyle with a slower pace of life. She owns and runs a guesthouse, and she has created an organic garden. She lives a life consistent with her principles.

CESO in Canada provides support to developing countries on topics related to sustainable development, and this is the major mandate of the fundacion, so this was a good fit. Being selected to undertake this assignment in Pijao was my pathway to Colombia. Natalia Naranjo Ramos, the CESO country representative in Bogota, organized and planned all the CESO projects. Natalia was able to get them approved through the CESO Canada office. She is a highly intelligent lady and does an excellent job for Canada.

The CESO Assignments—A Sustainable Tourism Action Plan for Pijao

The first CESO assignment I undertook in Colombia was entitled "A Sustainable Fair Trade Tourism Action Plan for Pijao, Colombia." It was like the previous assignments I had completed for CESO, related to tourism planning in the

Philippines—Lucban (2012) and Alabat Island (2015). To me, this project was like Babe Ruth hitting the ball out of the park. A well-articulated assignment, a committed sponsor—Fundacion Pijao Cittaslow, tremendous participation within the community, and combined with a series of tours throughout the region. There was full cooperation from all involved. A seventy-seven-page report was completed containing an action plan, full SWOT analysis (strengths, weaknesses, opportunities, and threats), recommendations, actions, priorities, monitoring and evaluation, sustainability provisions, and fair-trade checklists. It was well received, and I think a big reason an expanded Partnership Action Plan (PAP) evolved following this assignment.

The Partnership Action Plan (PAP)

Through discussions with Natalia, the country representative for CESO, we identified the need for many more projects in Pijao. This evolved into the PAP which contained seven new projects, all related to promoting sustainable development in Pijao, consistent with the mandate of the fundacion and the international Cittaslow movement. The PAP was approved in the CESO Office in Toronto, and I was selected to be the lead volunteer advisor. This resulted in three additional project trips to Pijao, Colombia between 2016 and 2019. The PAP assignments, in addition to the initial tourism assignment, were water, solid waste management, the training of low-income people in organic farming, tourism marketing, and strengthening the administrative practices of the fundacion.

What was identified during the initial visit to Pijao, and the follow-up PAP visits was the need for the fundacion and the town to work together on this project because the sustainable development vision would involve the town as well. It looked as if it would be an incredibly positive partnership. When leaving for Canada, the mayor of Pijao gave me a gift. It was a bottle of Aguardiente, the local whisky, which was appreciated. In return, I gave him a Canada hat, pin, and large Canadian flag.

Working with the Municipality

As things turned out, the town did not sustain a full commitment to working as a diligent partner with the fundacion. The mayor and the town staff were always busy with other priorities. From what I could determine, the leadership model of governance in Colombia vested a lot of authority with the elected officials. That is, they did not engage or coordinate actions with other organizations. In Colombia, inclusive consultations are not part of governance, as they are in Canada. There also seemed to be some tension between the Mayor and Monica as well. As a CESO lead volunteer advisor (LVA) for sustainable development programs in Pijao, it was a lesson learned - trying to push for and sustain that coordination was probably asking too much. I had been too optimistic, thinking I could engage the town as a strong participant, along with the fundacion.

But in the four years of CESO involvement with the fundación, the CESO volunteer advisors working under that PAP framework did some splendid work. It was a pleasure to collaborate with them as the LVA. Those skilled volunteers, who included Henning Rasmausson, Abhay Tadwalkar and Marie Andre Boucher, provided technical reports and advice on water management, solid waste management and recycling. organic agriculture, and marketing tourism. The reports were all well received by the fundacion.

The CESO work and documents are on record at the municipality. They may be of considerable technical benefit to the officials running the town if they chose to use them. This was a free consulting service for them, and I hope many recommendations eventually get recognized and are implemented in Pijao. They will be of use to the fundacion within their mandate moving forward.

The High Andes Mountains and the Coffee Growers

Because sustainability is the major emphasis of the fundacion, tours of local agriculture (especially coffee growers), local infrastructure, environmental conditions, and of course, eating healthy local cuisine were a priority. The first order of business was to view and investigate the growing of Arabica beans, the high-quality Colombia coffee grown on the slopes of the Andes Mountains, opposed to the lower quality Robustica, which is grown at lower, flatter elevations. To me, Colombian Arabica is absolutely the best coffee in the world. But, oh my god, the first tour was a drive high up into the Andes Mountains to visit organic farmers and the expert coffee growers. Those roads were so narrow, scary, and in poor condition. Up so high, I did not want to look down! How could anyone drive on roads like that so high up in the mountains? There were huge potholes and rocks sticking up everywhere, but despite those challenges, I loved those powerful panoramic views of those Andes Mountains. They were stunning.

For the field trips, myself, my son Lance, and several fundacion members, piled into Jeep Willy's, which were locally referred to as Yipaos. These were the high mountain four-by-four vehicles driven by the coffee farmers. Despite the bumps and the rough ride, we overcame the conditions and eventually, we got accustomed to those roads. That was the sacrifice you had to make to go to the area where the best coffee in the world is grown. The coffee growers we met were amazing, and the day was *fantastico! (*fantastic*)*

Lance and I encountered security guards at some of the farms, and despite the uniforms and weapons, they were extremely friendly. I was told their presence was part of the Colombia Drug Eradication Program, an eight-billion-dollar program with major funding from the USA. Colombians welcome and appreciate the security presence, as the country has experienced a lot of dangerous circumstances over the past few decades. At the Armenia Airport, during the security search, the officer told me, "Do not worry sir, this security is how us Colombians are taking back our country."

The coffee triangle is a place I had never heard of, but it is a place I think everyone would like to see. Coffee in Colombia is like religion. There is passion, commitment, and precision put into the coffee growing and production process. Monica and some Fundacion members, along with Lance and I, went to the remote places, to extremely high mountains, and we saw those coffee growers in action. In particular, the masters of the trade, the mentors to the coffee growers in Quindio Province–Don Leo (Don Leo Café Especial) and Jesus Pedraza (La Granada Café Gourmet), both from the Pijao area. They are regarded as the ultimate authorities on growing high quality, organic coffee, the best coffee in the world. They are the "best of the best"—the Wayne Gretzky's of the coffee world. Juan Valdez was the most well-known poster-boy for Colombian coffee for many years. He passed away in 2019. Don and Jesus are now the benchmark for setting the highest bar, and they are the next stage in the evolution of coffee. My son Lance and I saw these guys, spent time with them, and have pictures taken with them—the experience forever to be treasured.

The Secret of Growing High Quality Organic Coffee

Don and Jesus are specialty organic coffee growers. Every element in their coffee production cycle is carefully planned, a high level of quality control and emphasis on excellence in product development. To highlight the coffee process, bean seeds are selected carefully stemming from skill and insight developed from generations of family farming. The bean varieties grown are mostly Caturra and Castillo, and they need to be picked at the right time for ripeness. The beans are developed for excellence in taste, and for developing resistance to bean leaf disease. The expert growers use inter-cropping farming methods opposed to mono-cropping, as this is essential for organic production and ensures the soil stays rich over time. It also provides a natural protection against insects and plant disease. Intercropping generally means planting a variety of crops in the farmed area, such as banana and some deciduous trees for shade at the higher levels, the many coffee shrub plants mid-level, and vegetable root crops such as beans (frijoles), carrots (zanhorias), potatoes (patatas), garlic (ajo), chili (chiles), or other herbs or spices close to the ground.

Coffee beans are picked regularly and sorted by colour of ripeness and grade. In some other areas where coffee is produced, large-scale bulk coffee producers pick less frequently and short-cut the process by roasting all coffee beans at various ripeness levels and at higher temperatures. This is less work, but it results in a lower quality coffee taste. For growers like Don and Jesus, they stress excellence in coffee production. The beans are washed, and then dried through a natural solar process on sliding rooftops above the buildings or on the ground on mats – like how the Filipinos dry their rice. The beans are then washed again, varying periods of time, and then roasted. They are then bagged either as coffee beans or ground. Now you know the special secrets of organic Colombian coffee.

Sustainable Land Management in Agriculture

I observed some notable examples of sustainable agriculture in the remote coffee growing areas of Colombia. Jesus does high volume composting on his finca (farm), and nothing is wasted. Plant wastes, cattle and animal feces, and household food waste are all used in the process. The composted product—soil, then gets reused in farming. Don Leo uses a bio-mass process where he has a huge digester membrane where animal wastes are mixed with household and plant wastes, and the result is the production of methane gas used in cooking, lighting, and for supplemental energy at the finca. There are no public incentives or subsidies involved, just the will to use and re-use the resources wisely. I was amazed. In North America, we are not as motivated to use resources so wisely as this.

Our North American lifestyle is more focused on high levels of consumption without consideration of the harmful impact this is having on our environment or on future generations. In my view, many in rural areas of Colombia are doing it better. There are lessons to be learned from Colombia. There will be "hope for our world" when there is less waste and better use of our resources.

The Yipao Festival in Armenia

A tribute to the coffee industry in Colombia is the Yipao - Jeep Willy ten-day festival held each year in October in the capital city of Armenia, Quindio. This is a unique celebration, which I attended with my friend Ivan Restrepo. I met Ivan on the flight from Bogota to Armenia (enroute to Pijao) in October 2016. I have become exceptionally good friends with Ivan since that time. Ivan took me to this large celebration that had 106 Yipaos in the parade. Instead of floats as we normally see in a parade, there were Yipaos loaded with supplies, each one unique and different. The different kinds of cargo on board included coffee, agricultural products such as fruits or vegetables, household items, firewood, and more. The parade pays tribute to the rural coffee growers who grow coffee and other agricultural products in the Andes Mountains. They cannot survive at those high altitudes without a 4x4 vehicle, and for sixty years the vehicle of choice has been, exclusively, the Yipao. In the parade and interspersed with the loaded vehicles were marching bands, dancers in traditional costumes of

Colombia, horse riders, and military personnel, with music playing. This is a celebration only experienced in the coffee triangle of Colombia. It was *fabuloso* (fabulous)!

The National Coffee Park (Parque Nacional del Café)

In February 2016, my son Lance and I visited the National Coffee Park, which is in Monenegro, just six miles outside of Armenia. This is one of the Colombia's top tourist attractions. Information at the park indicated that it receives over 1 million visitors a year. The coffee park contains a museum, with exhibitions detailing the history, culture, and process of growing and producing coffee in the region. There is also an amusement park with rides and shows, as well as lots of food and souvenirs. The park areas are linked by gondolas. Lance and I found the park interesting, and we were able to obtain statistical and historical information on Colombia's coffee industry. However, after having already visited coffee farms of Jesus Pedraza and Don Leo (and some other coffee producing fincas); we had already received intimate and authentic information on coffee and its production from the grand masters of the trade.

Lance and I had a moment of panic at the National Coffee Park. After our driver dropped us off at the entrance, there was nobody in the entire pavilion who spoke English, and Lance and I both spoke extremely limited Spanish. We experienced hopeless confusion and a language barrier while at the entry gate. Finally, Lance found a person who spoke French. Lance was able to get all the information needed from him. It was a good thing Lance had taken French immersion education in Canada. It served us well and we were allowed to enter the park and to find the location where we were supposed to be picked up, so we could return to Pijao, otherwise - we still might be in Armenia.

Sustainable Urban Gardens in Pijao

There are many people within the town of Pijao, gardeners who raised animals, especially chickens, on very small properties. Many were members of the fundacion. They harvest vegetables and fruit, and herbs and spices, and they raise chickens for their own food security. They would sell their surplus to local supermarkets or from kiosks in the central plaza. These gardens are organically grown, and chickens are raised in a free-range manner. There was also a group of ladies who also grow flowers for export to larger centers in Colombia, all from small plots of land in the town. I was impressed by how efficient these small producers could be—Colombian gardeners are *asombroso* (amazing)!

Horses – Still Important in Rural Colombia

Rural Colombia still embraces the cowboy lifestyle of riding horses. Some folks ride their horses (with or without attached carts) into town and hitch them in front of stores, restaurants, or bars. The horses sometimes share parking spaces with cars, trucks, or motorcycles—this is acceptable in small towns like Pijao. It was very noticeable on the streets surrounding the central plaza.

Lance and I decided we would hire a guide to take us on a short trail ride. There was a party of eight of us. Before I knew it, we were on a trail going across *Rio Lejos* (Far Away River) and up the Andes Mountains. What I expected to be a twenty-minute ride, turned out to be a few hours. Crossing the river – *Rio Lejos*, I think was exactly how John Wayne or Clint Eastwood did it in a cowboy movie, and perhaps Indiana Jones did that as well. I never thought Lance and I would be doing something like that. The ride up into the Andres was quite dramatic. As we got higher, the trail began to get narrower and narrower. One side of the trail was a drop of several hundred feet straight down. A man with a horse-drawn cart with milk containers passed us, travelling in the other direction. Horses made routine deliveries of milk and supplies to the mountain dwellers. This caused us to ride even closer to the edge. Despite my sudden anxiety attack, we were fine. For my Colombian friends who lived in the Andes, this was not a big deal. For Lance and me, we were hanging on for dear life. But I must say, we encountered a surge of excitement. I would certainly do that again if I had the opportunity.

The Heritage of Colombia Architecture

Latin America and Colombia have a unique and fascinating culture. I had the opportunity to be exposed to the architecture and people involved in some innovative construction. I met Nestor Narvaez, an architect who had done architectural design work in Pijao, Armenia, Bogota, and in Panama. Nestor spoke no English, and I spoke little Spanish, yet we became good friends. I made a point to visit him each time I was in Pijao. Monica Florez, and my son Lance and I, had a dinner in his home in 2016. Nestor was eccentric, and he did not design conventional buildings. He showed me his portfolio of work, always building in harmony with nature. He showed me homes he had designed, which were constructed integrating existing trees in the middle of a building. Although unconventional, this was creative, unusual, but looked attractive.

My good friend Ivan Restrepo (who I mentioned earlier in this chapter), who was a tourism and hospitality advisor in Colombia, took me to his home in Calacara, Quindio, which is a small city located between Pijao and Armenia. Ivan was the project manager for the renovation of a rehabilitated boutique hotel in Calacara. Ivan took me on a tour of the building while it was under construction. The building had been in rough shape, but it had been gutted and was being redeveloped. His work entailed retaining the Latino heritage style of the building, while incorporating magnificent skylight features and mezzanine rooms on the upper floors. Ivan has told me that the project is now completed, and I am sure it is now an immensely popular boutique hotel.

Teaching English to Students in Pijao

While I was working with the fundacion group, a schoolteacher by the name of Gustavo, asked me to come to his evening class, where he was teaching young students how to speak English. On two of my visits to Pijao, he asked me to talk to his class—in English of course. I agreed to do that and on the visits in October 2016 and May 2018, I helped teach this conversational class. The kids ranged in age from ten to sixteen. They all responded well to my teaching, and there was a lot of participation. It was fun for me as well. The students were all very curious about life in Canada.

Coffee Fincas Being Sold for Avacado Production

In the coffee triangle, I was informed about a big emerging issue. There was a trend occurring where coffee lands were being phased out of production due to their replacement by other intervening crops, particularly hass avocado. Avocados are in huge demand in North America and Europe, but this story gets ugly. Avocados need high quantities of water, and they use non-organic chemical fertilizers to achieve a high level of production. In the coffee triangle, multi-cropping, low water use, and organic processes are more sustainable methods used by most coffee growers. I was told the high volume of avocado growing is starting to have harmful effects on the environment. To make matters worse, fundacion members told me that laundered money from drug lords of Mexico were the source for buying up coffee lands, and then cultivating those lands for avocado production. I was told that is because there is not land available for avocado growing in Mexico. Farmland is being purchased in countries throughout Central and South America for avocado production.

The passionate coffee producers and fundacion members are very disturbed over this trend. As part of my visits to the coffee farms, I was shown several examples of avocado acreages which were former coffee fincas. Many families in Pijao and throughout the Province of Quindio who have farmed coffee for generations are being bought out. What a shame to see this happen. These lands are arguably where the best coffee in the world is grown. Is the UNESCO designation of Colombia's Coffee Cultural Landscape going to be in jeopardy? Can this coffee culture survive? That is now an emerging concern in the Coffee Triangle.

Travelling to Manizales

I spent a week in Manizales, in the Province of Caldas, a city of about 435,000 people. [3] It is also located in the northern part of the coffee triangle, about a three-hour drive north of Armenia and more than four hours from Pijao. This city and surrounding region is extremely mountainous. There was a lot of turbulence at the airport. The landing of the Avianca Airlines airplane at the airport in 2019 was difficult and scary. The high altitude of the Andes Mountains had something to do with it. As I was settled in at the hotel, my daily routine involved walking from the hotel to the commercial area nearby.

This was quite a steep climb. Walking around, up, and down the hilly terrain, and the high-altitude, resulted in shortness of breath. This was an everyday occurrence getting around while in many areas of Manizales.

The CESO Assignment in Manizales—Actuar Microempresas 2019

I was asked to complete the final CESO evaluation report for the PAP program in Manizales because the lead volunteer advisor was not able to go at the scheduled time. Piggy-backing this assignment with my trip to Pijao in November 2019 was possible for me, so at the request of CESO, I agreed to do this. The host organization was called Actuar Microempresas, and their PAP contained six assignments. This was a non-profit lending agency that helped businesses acquire loan assistance for start-ups or expansion. I spent a lot of the time with Natalia, the country representative for Colombia, and with a few the staff from Actuar Microempresas. The individual assignments and consequently, the evaluation I completed, went smoothly. The staff, which included Juan Manuela Zuluaga, one of the vice presidents at Actuar Microempresas, were all extremely hospitable. The final monitoring and evaluation were completed without complications, and this PAP assignment evaluation was well received.

Touring Villa Maria and a Sports Bar Near My Hotel

The hosts in Manizales provided me with a very enjoyable schedule for my visit. First, I viewed the downtown, the central plazas, some artistic statues, and Christmas decor. I went across a very steep ravine on a gondola to Villa Maria, a small Latino town close to Manizales. It was a genuinely nice community with friendly people.

After that excursion and near to the hotel where I was staying, I noticed an open-air sports bar which extended right up to the sidewalk and next to the bus stop. City planners would refer to this as a "zero lot line" development. This enabled passers-by to grab a beer on the run. However, one evening after supper, I noticed a live soccer game, a World Cup qualifying match between Colombia and Ecuador, on the large TV screen in the bar. The bar was quite full, but I found a chair. The game was exciting and despite a bit of fear about being in a bar alone and not speaking much Spanish, I sat down and ordered a beer and watched some of the game. Colombia won 2-0, and everyone was extremely happy. There was no danger at all—if you were cheering for Colombia, which I was. People were friendly, and I walked home laughing about what I had done. The streets in the area were well lit and safe going back to the hotel.

The National Strike and Protests Throughout Colombia in 2019

There was an Indiana Jones adventure in Manizales, and in other parts of Colombia, during the week of November 18 to 23, 2019, when a national strike was declared in the country. This was because of the actions of President Ivan Duque Marquez, who was elected in 2018. I was told that Colombian's felt betrayed by him. A large monetary peace settlement had been negotiated with a rebel group called the Farc. This revolutionary group funded operations from the drug trade in Colombia. A peace deal was made with the Farc, and the Farc were granted compensation in exchange for peace and suspension of any of their unlawful activities. Many Colombians did not like that any kind of deal with a violent group involved with illegal drugs and violence. The president's actions were seen to be aiding and abetting criminals in the country instead of providing strong law and order as promised in the 2018 election.

Every night during my week in Manizales, I heard a noise at around nine p.m. It was a clanging of pots and pans that lasted for about thirty minutes. This was part of the protest and national strike occurring everywhere in Colombia. One evening I was having supper in a restaurant, and I was about to return to the hotel two blocks away. There was a lot of disruption happening on the main street. A police force was assembling on horseback, in helmets with shields, guns and batons. The horses began to march in unison down the street, from the front of the restaurant and toward the university. After the supper, I went outside, and a few blocks away I could see tear gas smoke bombs, and there was some crowd noise. As the horses went past, I crossed the street and there was Natalia Naranjo, the CESO CR for Colombia, and her husband looking to fetch me and take me to the hotel safely. That was an Indiana Jones experience that could have escalated into something serious but thankfully, it did not. The television news reported some violent incidences throughout other places in Colombia at that time. It was fortunate that things stayed more peaceful in Manizales.

Stores near that area closed and locked their doors, and some nailed sections of plywood over their windows as protection from vandalism. Fortunately for Manizales, the conflict did not get too bad. In Bogota, Cali, and some larger centers, the protests got violent. I was so relieved to make it back to my hotel room that night. That situation had not been anticipated.

The Usequen Market in Bogota

During my four trips to the coffee triangle, I did have some layover time in Bogota, a city of just under Eight million people. [4] Before I travelled to Bogota, I had the impression that this was a huge city rampant with crime, drugs, and violence, and that I should be afraid of this place. That was not the case at all from the experiences I had while there.

Natalia Naranjo, the CESO CR, booked at a boutique hotel, Casa Usequen for, in the Usequen area of Bogota. This is a good area next to a large plaza, embassy buildings, and a mall. Every Sunday there was a market, with crafts, souvenirs, artwork, and other goods for sale. I was able to go to that market in 2016 and 2019. Seller booths are set up around the local plaza, and they also extended outward along the narrow connecting streets, some of which get closed off. At that market, I purchased special belts made of cloth, souvenirs, small artworks, and some other things unique to Colombia. There were also Venezuelan immigrants at the market selling things, as many escaped the chaotic situation in their country to take refuge in Colombia. Some were selling keychains and wall hangs. I could not believe that many items were made from their local Venezuelan currency. They actually earn more money transforming their money into craft souvenir items, than spending it. I saw a souvenir Canadian flag made from Venezuelan pesos for sale, which was rather weird.

Touring Monseratte in Bogota

I was able to go to Monseratte in October 2016, where I took the rail car high up through a tunnel, which advanced to a mountain plateau overlooking

Bogota. There was a long boardwalk lookout, and a chapel at the top, where there were also many shops, bars, and restaurants. It seemed like I was close to heaven up there. The view of the huge metropolis of Bogota was spectacular. The altitude at Bogota was extremely high, but at Monseratte it was even higher, and I felt noticeably short of breath there, as I was not used to such a high altitude. If you are visiting Bogota for the first time, Monseratte should be the first order of business, it was *esplendido* (splendid)!

Visiting Candelaria in Bogota

After my visit to Monseratte, I travelled to Candelaria, the historic downtown of Bogota. Sebastien Castro, my guide, took me on a lengthy walking tour. He was a knowledgeable and helpful guide. The tour included the central plaza and cultural centre, and narrow, mostly brick and cobblestone streets in that area.

This historic area has incredibly special architecture. The old houses, churches, and buildings have Spanish Colonial baroque and art deco style representations. The area contained several universities, libraries, museums, and boutique shops.

Bolivar Square, the central plaza and surrounding cultural centre, dates back several centuries, and it is significant in the country's administration. Public protests take place there, and it is also the location for many ceremonies. I saw a military museum, Museo Botera del Banco de la Republica (cultural museum), and the Art Gallery of Fat People. The square was frequented by a few protestors, regular folks, and . . . pigeons. The surrounding buildings contained the legislature, the presidential palace, Bogota City Hall, and numerous other official governmental buildings. There was a lot of security, and many of the buildings and sites could not be accessed during the weekend that I was there.

Towns in the Coffee Triangle

I visited a few other small centers in Colombia's coffee triangle. These were Finlandia, Salento, Cordoba, and Buena Vista. They are all smaller communities between 5,500 and 8,000 in population, [5] similar in size to Pijao, the home-base for me during most of my time spent in Colombia. They are all centers for agricultural trade, but some are emerging as tourist hubs.

Finlandia already has retail shops offering souvenirs, classic Latino architecture, and beautiful crafts, located around an attractive plaza. Significant upgrades have been made to the plaza in recent years. It was a pleasant and attractive community.

Salento is more of a back-packers paradise, and it is often very crowded. This is a mecca for youth on their school breaks, as it is known for parties and fun, some of it legal.

Cordoba is less established as a tourism centre, but it provides goods and services for residents in the town and the surrounding area. It has an incredibly unique plaza with a circular activity area, frequented by kids on bikes and skateboards, playing basketball, and participating in other activities. The round shape provides a convenient view of goings on, as well as easy monitoring of children.

The shangri la of these small places for me is Buena Vista. The town is so exceptionally beautiful, high up in the Andes Mountains, with the most scenic views you can imagine. There is the San Alberto Café and Hacienda (a large farm or finca), where one can have a coffee and look at the town below, and far beyond. From the Hacienda, you can look endlessly from the mountains to the lowlands and many other communities far away in the distance. You can do specialty coffee tasting with experts at the cafe, and you can tour the surrounding lands growing the coffee, and then observe the processing as it occurs. It is a very classy place for tourists and coffee lovers. Buena Vista has a beautiful plaza surrounded by retail shops, and it is the main place for community activities. All of those towns had very attractive central plazas. The town of Buena Vista is extra special to me. This place is magic, and it puts a chill down my spine whenever I am there, as I was in 2016, 2018, and again in 2019.

Travelling between Pijao and Buena Vista—My Unexpected Adventure with Fernando

On a free day in October 2018, while working in Pijao, Fernando Uran of the fundacion was my guide going to Buena Vista. We traveled, had a meal, and then enjoyed an afternoon there. But in Indiana Jones movies, there are always unanticipated adventures. Because it was a Sunday, there was no bus returning to Pijao that evening. Although it was only eight kilometers to Pijao on a narrow road, you must go over a very steep mountain, so Fernando and I decided to walk there. Fernando was younger and more fit than I am, and he convinced me it should be no problem. Numerous coffee fincas were located along that route as well. I forgot how the high altitude can affect one's breathing, and after each kilometer it got more and more difficult for me, and my heart was pounding. But the views were spectacular and the experience memorable for sure. Just like Indiana Jones, I prevailed. Although I was exhausted, Fernando and I made it back safely to Pijao as it was getting dark. Fernando was my savior that day.

Lost in the Andes Mountains—Lance's Unexpected Adventure with Fernando

Fernando Uran was an active guy—an avid cyclist, and he was in good physical condition. One afternoon in 2016, when I was working on my CESO assignment, my son Lance did not have anything to do, so Fernando invited him to join his group of cyclists on a mountain ride. Lance was happy to get the invitation and agreed to go with them. However, after some time, the cycling group got quite far ahead of Lance, and he was left far behind and alone on the mountain road, not knowing where he was, for an hour. It was getting dark. A very scary situation—lost in the Andes Mountains of Colombia. Thankfully, the cyclists found Lance on their return ride, and he made it back to Pijao safely. He was very, very tired after that, and it is an event he will never forget.

Exiles Now Returning to Their Homeland of Colombia

To spend time in the heart of Colombia as I did was a true reflection of what that country is all about. Colombians are mostly hard-working people with big hearts, who like to laugh and enjoy life in their communities with their friends and families. They do not enjoy politics or government affairs, but they grudgingly tolerate the institutions and the apparent imperfections. But things have been improving in the last number of years. I met many Colombians who had lost hope in their country, went abroad, and now have returned to the coffee triangle with new hope. There is a much higher level of safety and security now. Who would not want to return to this amazing country?

Jessica Ramirez worked in St. Louis in the USA for twelve years, returned home, and married a Colombian in her home of Pijao. They went on to operate a large and successful coffee finca, Casa de las Oigudeas, and in 2016, they invited Lance and I for a dinner, which we enjoyed.

After spending fifteen years in Winnipeg, Manitoba, Canada, Sandra Fajardo returned to Finlandia, and she now works in Armenia City Hall. She gave me a tour of the building and took me to Finlandia in 2016. Her mother even prepared a traditional meal for all of us.

Mauricio Vargas returned to Colombia after spending twenty-two years working in Prince George, British Columbia, and now he owns and operates a coffee finca near Pijao with his wife Victoria. I visited Mauricio's finca, Pole Pole, in 2019 and viewed the coffee production, and I very much enjoyed the hospitality at his home. Pole Pole Coffee is also exceptionally good as well.

Luis Velaquez spent ten years in Miami, Florida in the USA, then returned to Colombia, where he now owns coffee producing lands in Tolima and Pijao. I toured Luis's Pijao property; he cooked me an authentic organic Colombian meal and gave me a quick tour of Salento. After that, he dropped me off at the Armenia airport for my return to Canada. He was a tremendous fellow.

Stephan Rosiny, a German national, and his wife Cecile, originally from Cali, Colombia, were both highly educated with PhDs, working in the Foreign Affairs Department in Hamburg, Germany. They decided to abandon their high stress lives and invest in a coffee finca near Pijao. I met them at the guesthouse, where I was staying in Pijao in 2016. At that time, they were purchasing the finca, Café Rio Leos. I visited them upon my return to Pijao in 2018. The finca had been upgraded, and it was emerging as a highly successful finca operation. Unfortunately, on my return trip to Pijao in 2019, I discovered that Stephan and Cecile were separated, and their dream was not concluding as planned.

Colombia and the Coffee Triangle in the Rear View Mirror

In closing this chapter on Colombia, my impression is that this is a country that people used to want to run away from. It was a dangerous place, a land of limited opportunity, and people were leaving. Today, a different story is emerging. Colombia is beautiful, with a rich culture and very friendly and welcoming people. It still has problems and challenges, but I think the future will be bright.

It was a thrill for me to have spent time in Colombia and meet so many wonderful people in such an amazing country. I would love to return someday.

FOOTNOTES

1. Census of Colombia (2018), in Wikipedia
2. Clement Garavito, Colombian Geographical Society, Bogotá (2020)
3. Census of Colombia (2018), in Wikipedia
4. Census of Colombia (2018), in Wikipedia
5. Census of Colombia (2018), in Wikipedia

Pictures of Pijao, Colombia in the Coffee Triangle

From top left: CESO Assignment photo opp in Pijao; CESO Assignment session with Colombia CR and fundacion host; CESO work session; CESO Assignment SWOT session; CESO assignment – meeting with the town and fundacion; CESO in Pijao – exchanging gifts with the Mayor; Lance with his daughter Magdalen before his departure; Latino heritage architecture; Central plaza in Pijao; Lance and I with finca security; Panoramic view from Andes Mountains; High Andes Mountain landscape

Pictures of Pijao, Colombia in the Coffee Triangle

From top left: Field trip to Finca Gloria – Don Leo; My son Lance and I with Don Leo; My son Lance and I with Jesus Pedraza; Sorting of coffee beans; Coffee icon Don Leo grinding beans; A sliding roof for drying coffee beans; A bio-gas digester making clean fuel for electricity; Agricultural and food wastes composted; Composted material (soil) in barrels – Jesus Pedraza; Yipao Festival parade – Armenia City; Cultural dance in the parade; Yipao demonstration in the parade – "a wheely"

Pictures of Pijao and Others Areas in Colombia

From top left: The Nationale Parque de café; Gondolas overlooking the Parque de cafe; Pavilion – Parque de cafe; Urban farming – commercially grown flowers; Horses in Pijao; Lance and I on a Colombian trail ride; With Nestor Navaez – Pijao architect; Tourism expert Ivan Restrepo – Calacara; Latino-styled balconies; Teaching English in the Spanish school; Hass Avocado – threat to coffee crops; Mono-crop not multi-crop farming

Pictures in Bogota and Rural Communities in the Coffee Triangle

From top left: CESO photo opp – Manizales assignment; Panoramic view of Manizales; Colombian fruit for sale; Statues of Colombian history – Manizales; An evening walk – sloped streets of Manizales; Manizales street bar – soccer on the screen; High mountain coffee fincas; The hike with Fernando Uran; Finlandia town plaza; Cordoba town plaza; Buena Vista – Shangri La; Narrow tourist street in Salento

From top left: View from San Alberto Hacienda – Buena Vista; Coffee tasting – San Alberto Hacienda; Narrow road – Buena Vista to Pijao; Television view – violence at National strike November 2019; Panoramic view of Bogota from Monserrette; Candelaria – narrow lane streets in central Bogota; Government sector – downtown Bogota; Bolivar Square – Bogota central plaza; Art from Museo Botero; A street protest in Bolivar Square – Bogota; Art from Museo Botero (museum of fat people)

Chapter 10

ETHIOPIA

Assignments in Bahir Dar and Addis Ababa and
Exploring Parts of Ethiopia in 2019 and 2020

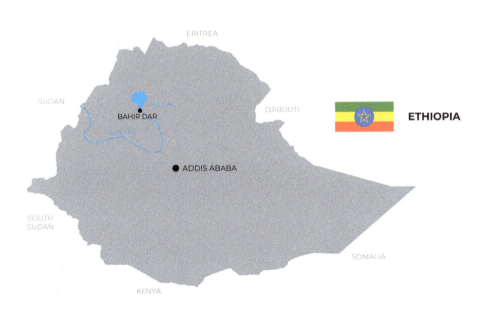

Map produced by Lance Smith

Ethiopia Background

Ethiopia is in East Africa, in the area geographically referred to as the "horn of Africa". It is located south and east of Sudan, south of Eritrea, west of Djibouti, south and west of Somalia, and north of Kenya. It has a 2019 population of approximately 112.08 million, up from the 2015 estimate of 98.9 million. The capital city is Addis Ababa, with a population listed as just under eight million. [1] After spending two weeks in that city, it felt huge. Ethiopia is the most populous landlocked country in the continent of Africa. It has one of the highest poverty levels in the world, and is also considered one of the most under-developed nations. Ethiopians are proud to tell you that they are one of two African countries never colonized. It was under communist rule from the 1970s to 1992. There have been tensions among tribal groups for many years, which are of concern in some areas of Ethiopia. Some of these tribal group's fear that governing with an emphasis on national unity, threatens their autonomy. Canadian's travelling to Ethiopia need to pay attention to the Canada travel advisory, since at times there could be conflicts in certain areas of the country.

Travelling to Ethiopia—Not as Planned

I travelled to Ethiopia in both 2019 and 2020, to undertake two CESO assignments. In 2019, it was my first time travelling to Africa. I was originally scheduled to travel from Canada to Addis Ababa, Ethiopia on February 25, and return to Canada on March 10, 2019. I left on schedule, but upon arrival in Frankfurt, Germany for a layover, I got extremely sick. I was in Germany for five days with my wife Clarita, but because of the illness, I decided to fly back to Canada with her. I did not proceed to Ethiopia at that time, and I requested that CESO reschedule the assignment.

Had I travelled on to Ethiopia at that time, I would have completed my CESO assignment on March 9, and the schedule would have had me flying out the next day—March 10. Instead on returning home that day, I had contemplated taking a flight from Addis Ababa to Nairobi, Kenya to go on a safari tour to view lions, tigers, elephants, and zebras in the wild. Had I done that, I would have been booked on the Ethiopian Airlines Flight 302. That 737 Max 8 flight crashed after taking off from Addis Ababa Bole International airport, and all 157 people on board died. The 737 Max 8 aircraft was grounded worldwide after that accident and not deemed safe to fly for almost two years' time. Serious modifications had to be made to that aircraft system.

Life is full of unknowns, fluke circumstances, and good or bad luck. I think about that event often, and I realize that it could have been me on that flight. I count my blessings—I am alive and well. Just like Indiana Jones, an instance where I escaped with my life, after a twist of fate.

CESO Assignment in Bahir Dar—2019

The CESO assignment in Ethiopia was rescheduled for March 28, 2019. I recovered from that flu back in Canada, and then departed from Kelowna, traveled to Calgary, and then to Frankfurt on Air Canada. The next leg was to Addis Ababa via Lufthansa Airlines. After a short layover, I travelled to Bahir Dar in northern Ethiopia, on Ethiopian Airlines. I stayed there on the assignment for two weeks.

Bahir Dar, located in northern Ethiopia, has a population of just under 800,000[2] and it is the capital city of the Amhara Region (Province). It is located next to Lake Tana, the second largest lake in Africa and the endpoint of the Nile River. I stayed at the Jacaranda Hotel, which was across the street from Lake Tana, and the view was fabulous. It was a basic hotel, but quite nice and comfortable.

The Urban Development Issues Assignment

I was selected to work with the Amhara Region (Province), for the Department of Urban Development and Housing. The assignment topic was to assess the growth taking place in that region, and the various problems and challenges associated with that growth. I was also asked to train staff, if possible, on upgrading work protocols. As an urban planner, I was comfortable with the assignment as described. I was looking forward to it. Belay Abate, CESO Ethiopia Country Representative, had done a fine job of organizing things. Shortly after I arrived, I met with the official responsible for the work program.

The purpose of the meeting was to coordinate the week's activities and ensure a schedule was followed. But there were several surprises.

Surprise number one—I thought I would be making an introductory presentation on the Monday morning, and then a final presentation at the end of the program. I had submitted the schedule in advance, and it had been approved. Not so, or perhaps it had been an error in translation, however, I was told they wanted me to provide presentations to different departments, on different topics, every day for the first week. Well, I had prepared one general presentation in advance. They subsequently advised me about the respective audiences – and I could see they needed five different presentations on specific topics. I had a lot of work to do "on the fly."

Surprise number two—I was told I would be picked-up on the first day (Monday) just before three p.m. They did not advise me that there was something called "East Africa National Time," which is six hours earlier than international time, so the pickup time was actually for nine a.m. international time. I was not expecting to be picked up that early, but I got ready "on the fly" again.

Surprise number three—I assumed the power-point projector could hook-up to my laptop. As I began to get ready for the presentation, the connecting cord did not fit into that projector. There was almost an hour delay, and finally a different laptop was made available. By using a memory stick, we were able to get the presentation underway.

Surprise number four – For the second day presentation, I was to be picked-up at nine a.m. international time again. I waited in the hotel lobby for my ride, but nobody came. After a few phone calls, a driver was sent to pick me up and take me to the presentation. I ended up arriving late, but it was certainly not my fault. Why did I not get picked up as scheduled? Well, that evening the official in charge of my transportation, a high-ranking government official, phoned me and wanted to have dinner at the hotel. I agreed. As we were eating, he apologized for not picking me up, humbly stating that his second wife—an unofficial wife, had been in labour having his child. He had a frustrated and apologetic look on his face, and he said, "My first wife, my official wife, is not happy with me, and I am having trouble keeping her happy." For the rest of the week, a driver was always on time to promptly take me where I needed to go.

The assignment in Bahir Dar went well, as far as identifying the problems and issues facing the city and the surrounding region. I worked with land administrators, engineers, policy makers, construction bureaus, division managers, and city planning staff from the city of Bahir Dar. I shared as much knowledge about the Canadian system of land management and planning as I could. However, it is unfortunate that the context of the assignment was not more clearly set out by the client. I think the Amhara officials wanted easy solutions and a clear path to fix the serious systemic issues and problems. What I gave them was a report and some guiding recommendations and directions for the future. The problems I saw them were:

- poverty
- shortage of housing
- large numbers of low-quality squatter housing
- unfinished buildings and construction
- a dysfunctional land management and leasehold registration system
- limited financial resources at all levels of government

The challenges in addressing these types of problems are overwhelming. Massive changes are necessary, and the changes need to be made through all relevant jurisdictions and all levels of government. I submitted a comprehensive report. I truly hope this wonderful country and the Amhara region can find a way to a brighter future and overcome these huge challenges; it will not be easy.

Surprise number 5—In the second week in Bahir Dar, after all the presentations were completed during the first week, the officials in charge had no plans for that second week. I had intended on completing a final report (which I did) and presenting it to the group, but the client indicated that other things were scheduled during the second week, so this would not be possible. Belay Abate, CESO CR for Ethiopia, when made aware of this, sent me to Bahir Dar University, where I spent a few days updating the translations of PhD research papers into an improved state of English. Some of the documents were not very understandable, and I was able to upgrade the English translations. The completed work was well received by those professors at the university. A few months after I returned to Canada, I received an email from the university advising me that one of those translated documents subsequently received major academic recognition. They thanked me for the assistance provided. That was very nice to hear.

CESO Assignment in Addis Ababa

Early in 2020, just before the Covid-19 pandemic began, I was in Ethiopia for a second time. The first week of my stay in Addis Ababa, the assignment was to work with the Ethiopian Women in Coffee (EWIC). I worked with Meseret Desta, the EWIC president, holding two workshops, and I assisted with the group in updating the strategic plan for that organization. Unfortunately, EWIC was mostly interested in finding markets for their coffee, with a path to coffee contract sales, and this was not my area of expertise. I was disappointed that I could not assist them with that. The CR Belay Abate assured me that there would be lots of work for me for the second week, and he set me up to work with another assignment for the Ethiopian Apiculture Board (EAB). Negash Bekema, the general manager, and his staff. The EAB were extremely keen on completing their strategic plan and extending it to 2024 and that was something that I could help them with. After a few intense sessions, the work was completed, and it was well received by the EAB. Working with those two - the EWIC and the EAB was very enjoyable.

Finding a Tour Guide in Bahir Dar

During the assignment in Bahir Dar in 2019, I was able to find Ashhenafi Merra, a tour guide at the hotel, who spoke English, which I could mostly understand. In Bahir Dar, the language barrier was huge. Even though I was told English was taught in the schools, other than a few people working in the hotels, communication was a major problem. Ashhenafi was efficient in organizing a Saturday boat tour on Lake Tana followed by a Sunday trip to the Blue Nile Falls. He greeted me prior to the tour in "the Ethiopian way"—shoulder to shoulder with a pat on the back.

Hippos

On our tour, we saw some hippos up close. We were in a smaller sized twelve-seater boat and were able to navigate quite close to the hippos, which was something special for me. The hippos would submerge for a bit, then abruptly surfaced. However, as we started to maneuver the boat near where we thought the hippos were, suddenly there was a loud thump at the bottom of the boat. A hippo banged his head into the boat as it was coming to the surface. Large animals such as these can capsize a boat quite easily, so that was an extremely dangerous and scary moment. The boatman immediately distanced the boat from where the hippos were swimming, and we had no further encounters. That was quite an episode.

Fishing in Lake Tana

Fishing is an important activity around Lake Tana. We saw a fisherman on the lake fishing in a unique boat made of papyrus. We saw huge flocks of stork birds along the shoreline, next to the main fisherfolk docks. There were fifteen or twenty open-air restaurants cooking the fresh fish. The fisher folk cooked fabulous grilled tilapia from those modest open-air shacks. It was the best meal eaten in Ethiopia. In fact, fish is the one main meal I really enjoyed. A lot of the local Ethiopian cuisine was too spicy and hot for my liking. But many people love this cuisine.

Blue Nile Falls

After the Saturday Lake Tana tour, my guide and driver took me to Blue Nile Falls on Sunday. The falls were only thirty-two kilometers from Bahir Dar but because of the rough dirt roads and the road congestion, it took almost two hours to get there. It was a hot and dusty day. The drive was an "eye-opener". There were many people walking on the road, carrying supplies on a long stick draped over their shoulders or a water container over their head. Sometimes they would rest under flat-top Acacia trees for shade and to cool-off. There were only a few of these trees scattered throughout that desert-like landscape. There were numerous horses and donkeys pulling carts with food, supplies, or water on the road. Cattle were also being herded along, sometimes in the middle of the road, making it difficult for vehicles to pass.

Once arriving at the Nile River, we took a short boat ride to the other side, and then we walked about one and a half kilometers to the falls, a popular tourist destination. We were advised that the Blue Nile Falls are the second biggest waterfalls in Africa, next to Victoria Falls in Zimbabwe. During late February and in March, the Nile River at the Blue Nile Falls were at the lowest level, so I was not seeing them at the best time of year. I can imagine when those falls would be at full capacity. Despite that, they were still beautiful, and the experience was enjoyable. There was a hanging bridge over a deep-cut ravine. A person could walk on that bridge to the other side of the falls, then return, which I did. This reminded me of the Capilano swinging Bridge in North Vancouver, Canada.

What is Khat?

On the trip to Blue Nile Falls, the driver pointed to a field growing khat—a narcotic plant that has been chewed and enjoyed socially for centuries in the Horn of Africa. It is the equivalent to marijuana in that part of the world. It is being discouraged now for use in Ethiopia, although it is legal. I was told these crops are sold and exported widely to the middle east, particularly Yemen. Khat is a valuable source of income for the farmers, and it provides economic benefits for the country, so the crop growing continues. Our driver stopped the vehicle and helped himself to some khat. He did not consume it while driving the vehicle, which was probably a good thing. He offered some to me, suggesting I chew it, but I decided that using a mind-altering substance in a foreign country – that was not a good idea.

The Habesha

While staying in Addis Ababa, I noticed that there were many billboards displaying a black, quite attractive, female face, and no words. It was a symbol of the Habesha ethnic group. The artistic symbol on many billboards reinforced the pride of the dominant culture within Addis Ababa. I found this quite very interesting.

Ethiopian Coffee Ceremonies

During both the 2019 and 2020 trips to Ethiopia, I experienced coffee ceremonies, an age old Ethiopian cultural tradition. In Canada, we may go to Tim Hortons or Starbucks for coffee and socialization, but in Ethiopia, it is somewhat of a spiritual occasion too. Coffee originated in Ethiopia, and in most households, a female member of the family conducts a coffee ceremony. Fresh flowers and grass are spread on the floor or ground, while burning incense (frankincense, myrrh, and sandalwood). This makes the air even more fragrant, due to the smoke which is generated. I experienced a coffee ceremony on several locations—indoors at the Best Western Hotel and at Mama's Kitchen restaurant in Addis Ababa, and outdoors near the Jacaranda Hotel in Bahir Dar and at the Azewa Mariam Monastery (the Hidden Monastery) on an Island in Lake Tana, as part of Ashenafi's tour. The ceremony near Lake Tana was very authentic. An Ethiopian family welcomed our group to a traditional coffee ceremony, where beans were roasted. They were then placed on a flat rock and crushed into grounds by placing another rock on top, and the rubbing effect of the two rocks on the beans produced grounds. These grounds were filtered, then boiled and brewed for drinking. The coffee was served in Ethiopian pots called *Jebana* which are unique as well, and have been used for centuries, I am told. My participation in the coffee ceremony on Lake Tana was a truly authentic event that I will not forget but these are an everyday routine cultural practice throughout Ethiopia.

Ronnie the Shoe Shine Boy

In returning to the Jacaranda Hotel, near the entrance was Ronnie, the shoe-shine boy. He was the happiest and friendliest guy I have ever met, continually making jokes, mostly in his native Amharic tongue, but he made foreigners laugh too. He told me he had eight children and supported them by shining shoes. He was hoping to have tourists as his customers. I was happy to get my shoes shined and contribute to Ronnie's income. It was nice to be around such a happy person as him.

Experiencing Ethiopian Culture

Ethiopians love music, singing, and dancing. In both 2019 and 2020, I was able to watch some remarkably interesting cultural music and dancing venues. I visited some popular restaurants in Bahir Dar, and later in Addis Ababa, and in both places, the restaurants provided cultural entertainment. This was certainly different from anything I had ever seen before. The main instruments used were a *masenqo* and a *krar*. The *masenqo* looks as if it would play like a violin, with a diamond shape at the base of the instrument. It has a unique sound, not at all like a violin. The *krar* looks like a harp with a holding apparatus at the top of it. It also has a unique sound, and not like a harp. The singing was a repetitious chanting sound but quite moving, and I liked it. The dancing routines were very interesting as well. The traditional costumes were accompanied by accessories or props such as spears and umbrellas, all depicting a proud history of the nation.

I learned something else about the Ethiopian culture. During my visit to Azewa Mariam Island on Lake Tana in 2019, I was walking past the numerous commercial kiosk stalls on a path to a monastery. While looking at some of the extremely attractive handicrafts and souvenirs, I casually suggested to a merchant that on the return from the monastery, I might buy some of those items. I was trying to be polite but did not actually intend to buy anything. Well, in returning down that path, I passed those kiosk stalls again and continued walking towards the boat. My tour guide Ashenafi stopped and retrieved those attractive items that I said I liked. For Ethiopians, my casual mention of a purchase was understood to be a commitment to purchase those handicrafts. So, in Ethiopia, particularly in the Habesha culture, integrity means that if you say or even imply you might do (or purchase) something – that means you are going to do it. A lesson learned. Yes, I did purchase the items.

An Ethiopian Wedding Reception

At the restaurant in Addis Ababa, it was a Saturday evening, so it was terribly busy. There was also a wedding reception going on. My hosts, the EWICA and I, observed this from a distance. There were speeches, and a jumping dance in a circle. It was interesting to see. Like weddings in Canada and elsewhere, weddings are a happy occasion for all in attendance.

Visiting Places of Worship

I visited and toured a few interesting places, including some impressive buildings and structures which were places for religious worship. Ethiopia contains the largest Orthodox Christian population outside of Europe. [3] I was told that Orthodox Ethiopians have much higher levels of religious commitment than Orthodox Christians in the faith's heartland of Central and Eastern Europe. It was quite apparent how seriously the people took their religion.

The places I visited included the Azewa Mariam Monastery—located on an island in Lake Tana in 2019, and the Bole Medhane Alem Cathedral in Addis Ababa in 2019, and a monastery located near the Debre Libranos in 2020. They were all serving the same function, places to worship and for spiritual events. However, architecturally, all these buildings were quite different. Some also contained larger compounds and were also places for the training of clergy, the education of children and for storing and displaying historic religious artifacts and artistic drawings.

Azewa Mariam Island Monastery on Lake Tana

At the Azewa Mariam Monastery in 2019, there was a complex of buildings, but most notably, a building of historical and religious artwork and archival records. It was quite amazing to see the artwork on the interior walls of that sacred building. I was not supposed to take pictures, but I mistakenly did, and my camera was taken from me until I left the building. There was a large religious session taking place outside, but I did not get pictures of that. The paintings were of significant religious importance, as Ethiopia claims to be the historical birthplace of world religions. I certainly got reminded of that at many sacred places throughout the landscape in Ethiopia. I cannot speak with a lot of expertise on these subjects, but the knowledge gained, and the overall experience was fascinating.

The Monastery in the Debre Libranos

On a tour near to the Great Rift Valley in 2020, I viewed the Monastery in Debre Libranos, I felt far out of my comfort zone. The guide, Frihoet Lemma, her son Jolsey, and I went to a museum within Monastery compound. To proceed further inside, the compound, a Monk asked us several questions:

First Question—Have you had sex in the past twenty-four hours? (If so, you cannot enter).

Second Question (directed to Frihoet)—Are you currently menstruating (If so, you cannot enter).

Third Question—Did you eat meat (beef, chicken, or pork) in the last twenty-four hours? (If so, you cannot enter).

We all passed the test questions and were allowed to enter the museum and the monastery complex. The museum contained documents (some dating back over 1000 years), ancient tools, household items, and many paintings, some similar to the those seen at Azewa Mariam Monastery a year earlier.

For the next part of the tour, the monk took us to the main church. There was intense worshipping taking place, as it was a religious holiday. Before entering, we had to take off our shoes and remove our hats. The men were located at more prominent spaces in the building, and the women were relegated to sections nearer to the back of the building. There seemed to be thousands of monks, high priests (I am not sure of the hierarchy or their titles), and regular people in that monastery. Everyone was dressed in the traditional Ethiopia garb. There was loud chanting and kneeling and lighting candles. I have never seen so many people crammed into a building. In Canada, the fire code would have been violated, but not here. Even so, many people could not get into the building, remaining outside, worshipping in the open square at the front of the church.

I felt claustrophobic, shoulder-to-shoulder and frozen to a spot but otherwise, it would have resulted in rubbing against or colliding with someone. This was very scary for me, the only Caucasian person amongst thousands, and the only person dressed in Western clothes. Although this was a memorable moment I will not forget, I was happy to leave this compound. I was uncomfortable and afraid the entire time I was in that complex. But the monk and Frihoet took good care of me and after twenty minutes, I exited the monastery and left the compound. My fear was not justified, and it was safe, but it was one powerful experience.

Melane Alem Cathedral

While in Addis Ababa in 2019, I also saw the Melane Alem Cathedral, as it was only a two block walk from the Best Western hotel where I was staying. There were two other CESO advisors, doing assignments in Ethiopia at that time. I seem to have forgotten their names. They were both returning to Canada the next day, but I was just beginning my stay in Ethiopia. We spent the afternoon together, walking around the downtown area of Bole near the hotel. That excursion included looking at the enormous and stunning Orthodox Christian cathedral, located within a large, landscaped park with numerous buildings on the site, some under construction. On that day only a few people were viewing the cathedral.

On the way back to the hotel, I got a bit too aggressive while taking pictures. I took a picture of a family walking in front of their tent-like house, and an angry man took exception to it, and he shouted at me. I had to respectfully apologize to him and stop taking random pictures without permission or it would have become a problem for me. This was my first day in Africa. It was a learning experience regarding the cultural norms and expectations regarding taking photos. That was not appreciated. You must always ask for permission.

The Great African Rift Valley

A tour was taken in 2020, where I travelled from Addis Ababa to the Rift Valley where I saw this phenomenal geological landscape. Near Debre Libranos, it is about a three-hour drive northwest of Addis Ababa. Wow, it was certainly worth seeing. Information on-site indicated the Great African Rift Valley is the name given to this very lengthy geographical trench, about 6,000 kilometers (3,700 mi) in length. Frihoet indicated that the trenches run from northern Syria in Southwest Asia, through Ethiopia and Kenya, to central Mozambique in East Africa. The rift is bordered by a series of mountains and active volcanoes that are thirty million years old.

My first impression was that I must have been on another planet. I saw part of the Grand Canyon in the United States many years ago, and the sharp drop-off to the valley was in some ways similar. It was so far down to the valley bottom. But at the top of the valley were the mountains, and they were like a straight horizontal line, as if created by human construction, but they were not. Frihoet the guide, her son Jolsey and I were able to take a two-kilometer hike on a trail along the edge of Rift Valley, and go down to the historic Portuguese bridge, which I was told was the oldest bridge in all of Africa. It was, of course, constructed by Portuguese in the sixteenth century.

Between Rift Valley and Addis Ababa were semi-desert lands being farmed mostly for grazing of forage or cereal crops. In early February, it was extremely dry and hot. These flat to rolling areas were a considerable contrast to the landscape of the Rift Valley.

Housing in Rural Ethiopia

In rural Ethiopia, there is limited technology or mechanization in play, so agriculture is a hard way to earn a living. The housing in rural areas of Ethiopia is very modest and simple. There are many people living in mud huts and tent-like structures. It is my understanding that there are no social safety nets or housing programs to aid the people who need assistance or who may be having difficulty finding adequate shelter.

Baboons

On the return trip from Debre Libranos back to Addis Ababa, there was a surprise. There were a lot of Chillida's baboons beside the road. I had the opportunity to get closeup and observe them in their habitat. This was quite exciting to see, and I was amazed at how many of them there were. They were not at all intimidated by the presence of humans. You could get quite near them, and they would not pay any attention to you. However, there was a caution to not get too close, as there have been instances where they attack humans if you intrude too close to their space.

Eating Dangerously

While on my own one day, I found a place across from the hotel that served chocolate milkshakes—one of my favourite treats to have back home in Canada. I consumed one, but within hours, I was violently sick.

Lissan Petros, who worked in the CR office in Ethiopia, came to my rescue and took me to a clinic the next morning. After a few tests in the clinic, I was given antibiotics, electrolytes for my dehydrated condition, and an antacid solution for my stomach. The antacid was from Egypt, and it worked amazing—that antacid is not to be found in Canada. After twenty-four hours, I was fine. The medical service at the Nordic Medical Clinic in Addis Ababa was excellent. A special thank you to Lissan. *Ameseginalehu* (Thank you)!

Dining with Fellow CESO Volunteers while in Addis Ababa

While staying in Addis Ababa in 2020, I met two Canadian volunteers, Andy Anderson from Victoria, and Paul Bennett from Ottawa. They were also undertaking CESO assignments in the city at the same time I was. We met in the hotel lobby each evening and went for dinner together. They both had greater culinary knowledge than I, so every night was a unique dining adventure—Yamani, Arabic, Italian, Greek, and French, as I recall. Some food was good, and some not so good for me. The local favourite Ethiopian food is injera, a flat spongy-like sourdough, served with meat and vegetables in a hot and spicy berber sauce. It was too much spice for my weak stomach. At times in Ethiopia, I had some trouble finding the kind of food that I wanted to eat.

It is always fun to have company while in a strange country, especially with Canadian friends to enjoy new experiences. Near our hotel, Paul informed Allan and I that he had been threatened and robbed, in daylight, in an area near the Best Western where we were staying. His wallet was discovered by police within two hours of losing it, with nothing missing except for a small amount of cash. That was fortunate. We all walked around that area every day, so that occurrence was a concern, although in daylight it was an unusual occurrence.

University Park

Paul, Allan and I went to the recently opened Unity Park, the major urban tourist attraction in Addis Ababa. It was located on a forty-hectare site near the centre of Addis Ababa, and it contained a wide range of things including wild animals, notably the rare black lion, the in famous symbol of Ethiopia. There was a large museum of artifacts and remarkable historical showcases on the political and religious history of Ethiopia, provided both in written and video form. There was an amusement park for kids, lots of food opportunities, and a beautiful park with trails for casual hiking. We spoke to other tourists from Germany, Holland, Italy, Turkey, Serbia, and Israel the day we were there. This was a delightful place to spend a Sunday afternoon.

Keeping Ethiopia Unified

Abi Ahmed has been the Prime Minister of Ethiopia since 2018. He initiated a platform to reduce poverty, improve human rights and enhance the economic progress in the country. Progress was being made on these fronts until the covid nineteen pandemic began. Even with these well-intended efforts, there have been continuing tensions among tribal and religious groups in that country, particularly involving the northern Tigray area in Ethiopia. The challenge to build bridges between different religious and ethnic groups throughout Ethiopia has been huge. Although Abiy received a Nobel Prize in 2019 for his efforts, conflict in that country seems to be increasing again.

During my stay, there was evidence of rebellion, even in Addis Ababa. On February 5, 2020, just before I departed from that city, there was a confrontation a few blocks away from the Best Western hotel where I was staying. The conflict was between citizens and police and stemmed from a disagreement over a religious issue. Some shooting occurred, and two civilians were killed, and shooting continued through the night. [5] I did not hear anything from my hotel room, but the next morning, some people were talking about the disruption that had occurred.

My taxi travelled through the area of conflict the next day, and it was shocking to see a huge presence of both city and federal police on both sides of the street, many displaying machine guns. The traffic was slow. I was happy when the taxi was able to move past that area of the city.

Missed My Flight—Oops

There were a lot of surprises in Ethiopia, and there was yet another on my departure. I completed the CESO assignment successfully with the Ethiopian Apiculture Board (EAB) on February 6, 2020. I left for the airport on the morning of February 7, and arrived at the airport for check-in at eleven a.m. My ticket showed the departure as one-twenty, but it did not say a.m. or p.m. I guess because my assignment finished later in the day on the sixth, I thought the departure would be one-twenty p.m. on the seventh, but that was the wrong assumption. At check-in, I was informed that I had missed my flight. I had ten minutes of crisis and panic. Then, I regained my composure and went about finding a way to get home.

Since the ticket had been booked through Air Canada, I was informed by Ethiopian Airlines that it needed to be re-booked through them. Air Canada does not fly into Addis Ababa, and there was no Air Canada counter in that airport. It took a while to for me to think clear. I caught my breath. I found a 1-800 number on the bottom of my ticket. Thank goodness that my cell phone was charged and working. Quite quickly, I connected with a lady in Canada from the travel agency who had booked my ticket. I was informed it was three a.m. in Canada. The lady at the other end was unbelievable, and she re-booked me on the next day's flight. The flight was the same flight itinerary, but just a day later, with a one-twenty a.m. departure. The rebooking charge turned out to be a minimal $150 fee. It was fortunate that I was an Air Canada Prestige 25k member. Sometimes, you get lucky. This situation was an example of tremendous customer service. The trip home was fine, and I was only delayed by one day.

Ethiopia in the Rear View Mirror

My memories of Ethiopia will last forever. Despite the surprises, it is a place full of very lovely people and beautiful places to see. There are many difficult issues facing the country, including religious and economic issues and political rivalries at play. In 2020, the leadership in place seemed to be moving forward with a vision to unite the country and improve economic and social conditions. However, conflicts within the country seemed to be brewing.

Ethiopia and the continent of Africa live a vastly different lifestyle than we do in North American. The religious chanting throughout the night is a reality. It is healing for the souls of the Orthodox Christians and Muslims who do it. It takes time to feel comfortable while there because everything seems so different, but with help and guidance from some trustworthy locals, this is a place to be enjoyed. I would love to go back again.

FOOTNOTES

1. World Population prospects – Population division, United Nations Department of Economic and Social Affairs, November 19, 2019, cited on Wikipedia

2. World Population prospects – Population division, United Nations Department of Economic and Social Affairs, November 19, 2019, cited on Wikipedia

3. Encyclopedia Britannica, Assistant Editor Melissa Petruzzello, July 20, 1998, cited on Wikipedia

4. Martina Stevis Grindneff, Nobel Peace Prize Awarded to Abiy Ahmed, Ethiopian Prime Minister, New York Times (October 11, 2019) article cited on Wikipedia

5. Addis Standard newspaper, Addis Ababa, February 5, 2020, cited on Wikipedia

Pictures of Bahir Dar and Lake Tana in Ethiopia

From top left: CESO Bahir Dar Assignment Photo Opp; CESO Bahir Dar session in 2019; CESO assignment photo with professors – Bahir Dar University; CESO Assignment photo opp – Women in Coffee – Addis Ababa 2020; CESO Assignment photo opp – EAB – Ethiopian Apiculture Board – 2020; CESO CR and Canadian Advisors; Addis Ababa 2020; Panoramic view of Bahir Dar and Lake Tana 2019; Unfinished Construction everywhere – Bahir Dar; Common toilet facility in Bahir Dar; Shoulder-to-shoulder greeting in Ethiopia; Tuk Tuk taxi service

Pictures of Blue Nile Falls, a Coffee Ceremony, and Other Ethiopian Events

From top left: Seeing a hippo in Lake Tana in 2019; A papyrus boat; A huge group of storks; The Portuguese Bridge – Rift Valley; Cultural attire and the rural setting; A group of Chilldas Baboons; Seeking shade under the Acacia Tree; Most people have to walk; Excitement at Blue Nile Falls 2019; Blue Nile Falls 2019; Preparing for an Ethiopian Coffee Ceremony; A field of Khat

Pictures of the Great Rift Valley and Addis Ababa

From top left: Eating Tilapia with Guide Frihoet; Eating Injera; Habesha culture on billboards; Ethiopian Music at the Cafe in Bahir Dar; Heavy traffic on a rural road; Ethiopian Wedding reception 2020; A Monk at the Azewa Mariam Island Monastery on Lake Tana; Artwork in the Monastery; The Debre Lebranos Monastery; Worshipping in the monastery; Present at intense worshipping at the monastery; Bole Medhane Cathedral

From top left: Impressive souvenirs and merchandise; Looking across the African Rift Valley; Another view from the Great Rift Valley; Ronnie the shoeshine boy; The daily hustle of city life; Moving supplies by donkeys and carts; A rural remote village 2019; Squatter housing in the city; Ethiopian historical artwork; Ethiopian artist selling his works; The Unity Park Pavilion – Addis Ababa; Artwork at Unity Park

Chapter 11

MONGOLIA

*The Mongolia Assignment and Exploring
a Frontier Like No Other in 2017*

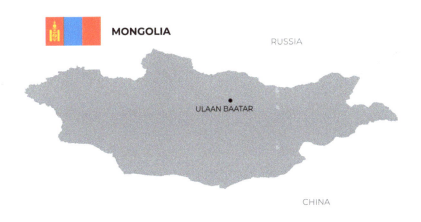

Map produced by Lance Smith

Background to Mongolia

Mongolia is a landlocked country located between China and Russia. It contains about 3.17 million people, almost half of which live in the capital city, Ulan Baatar. Mongolia has the lowest population density of all countries in the world at 1.7 people per square kilometer. The nation is about one and a half times the size of the province of British Columbia in Canada. [1] Genghis Khan is the renowned national hero, revered conqueror of the world and founder of the thirteenth-and fourteenth-century Mongol Empire. Forever, he is the undisputed champion of Mongolian culture and history. The airport in Ulan Baatar, streets, parks, the main plaza, food products, vodka, beer, energy drinks, businesses, buildings, the biggest national park—just about everything in Mongolia is named after Genghis Khan. Sometimes, strange as it seems, his name is spelled differently where it is used. I found that odd. In Canada, we worship our sports and particularly our hockey stars, but I think that pales in comparison to the mythology and hero-worship of Genghis Khan in Mongolia.

The CESO Assignment

I travelled to Ulan Bataar in October 2017, as I had been accepted for the assignment as part of the MERIT program – **M**ongolia **E**nhancing **R**esource Management Through **I**nstitutional **T**ransformation. MERIT was established by Global Affairs Canada, the branch of the Canadian government that provides international support and is part of CESO. As a CESO advisor, I was qualified for this assignment and was recruited by MERIT officials. The project topic was entitled, "Reviewing the Enforcement and Compliance Practices of Mining in Mongolia." As part of my working career in Canada, I had been responsible for the staff who enforced and secured compliance with building and development laws and regulations. Enforcement of mining was of a different nature, but because the principles of enforcement are universal, it was felt by MERIT that I could assess the procedures for mining. My proposed approach was to examine enforcement taking place and determine how effective the Mongolian compliance was, and then suggest improvements.

I arrived in early October. The weather was already cool, and it seemed just like the late fall weather in Manitoba, Canada. I was taken to the hotel where

I would be staying, called the Corporate Hotel, and it was quite comfortable. After a night's rest, I began a judicious process of examining the enforcement process. I interviewed officials involved with policy, environmental regulations, technical regulations, and the legal framework in Mongolia. All the people were courteous and intelligent; however, a number of problems were immediately apparent. Different agencies were overlapping in regulatory functions, causing confusion. The regulatory agencies were critical of each other, so they did not always work together on issues as a team, or in a coordinated manner. It was apparent that improvements were necessary.

There was a huge problem in executing this assignment. This assignment and assignments involving two other volunteers took place only a matter of weeks after the country's election. The outcome of the election was that there would be a transition to a change in government at the end of the year. Because of this the Mongolian officials I interviewed were cautious. I sensed everyone had an unquestioning respect for authority and a "steady as you go", and "don't rock the boat" mentality. My guess was that nobody wanted to lose their job. It soon became apparent that this was not the right time for assignments in Mongolia until the newly elected government became established in power.

I also had asked those in charge if I could be taken to the mine sites to observe some enforcement and compliance issues. I was informed that the cost, and schedule did not allow for this, so my request was denied. I also asked if I could look at some of the files related to enforcement. These files were confidential, and again my request was denied. It was clear to me that the content of the assignment could not be done as comprehensively as intended. In the end, a general report was prepared, the assignment completed early. The fundamentals of effective enforcement of regulations were articulated in the report. Election times are not good times to do policy related assignments, and make bold recommendations, either within Canada or abroad. I was a bit disappointed in that assignment outcome, but that is the way international work goes at times.

Mongolian Culture

On occasion, Mongolian's were wearing cultural dress or clothes that I had not seen elsewhere in my travels. In rural areas, many people live in ger huts—like a round igloo, but made from a thick tent-like material. There is a hole in the centre of the roof so that smoke from the wood burning for the heating and cooking can escape.

The Mongolian culture is unique. I was briefed on some cultural customs. For example, Mongolians never make eye contact. Also, they receive offerings with the right hand only, and sleeves should be rolled down.

The highest quality cashmere clothes in the world—coats, scarves, hats, and gloves, come from Mongolia. I went to some shops and brought a cashmere sweater home to Canada. Amazing merchandise!

Eating Horsemeat?

During my assignment in Ulan Baatar, I was working out of the legal office of the Ministry of Environment and Tourism. Two ladies were in the office, along with an interpreter who was assisting me. They came up to me and said it was lunch time and there was lots of extra food to share. They generously offered me horsemeat, mixed with some cabbage. Mongolians commonly eat a lot of meat, including horsemeat, as part of their diet. But eating a horse . . . that was something I could not do, so I politely declined. I am not sure whether Indiana Jones or Anthony Bourdain would have eaten horsemeat, perhaps they would have.

Batkhuyak—My Mongolian Colleague with Russian Connections

The person who provided most of the assistance to me during the assignment was Batkhuyak Naigal. His parents were of Mongolian and Russian descent. Batkhuyak was hired as a MERIT program officer, and he looked after me during my stay in the city, and he became a good friend. He was educated in Moscow and had worked for the Russian government for several years before moving back to Ulan Bataar, where he had been born and grew up. In addition to showing me how to eat Russian and Korean food, he gave me insight into how the Mongolian people think. Even though communism ended in 1990, Russians were still highly regarded in Mongolia, and it appeared that Mongolians had a good relationship with Russia, more so than with China.

Batkhuyak considered Vladimir Putin a great builder and leader of Russia. He believed that Russia was misunderstood in the Western world and was always the default scapegoat by the USA, which he considers unfair to Russians. It was a different perspective than the North American characterization of Russia. I have always felt uncomfortable with Putin, but Batkhuyak was a decent guy and I did not argue with him.

Ulan Bataar—Many Positive Urban Planning Features

I am an urban planner, and so I am often looking at things from a livability perspective. There were many city planning design features of the Soviet era evident in Ulan Baatar, and they were interesting. There was a lot of attention paid to pedestrian spaces and mobility, nice parks, and playgrounds, as well as neighbourhood and civic plazas. It was a very relaxing and enjoyable experience to walk on wide sidewalks and have comfortable separation from vehicles, and I believe these elements should be replicated more in North America. However, there was a dark side in their planning. Parking and traffic were a huge problem . . . a nightmare. Cars were double parked, sometimes parking in public spaces that were not designated for this. It was better to walk a few kilometers rather than take a taxi. Traffic congestion and the associated pollution were stressful and unhealthy. Parking and traffic planning got failing marks from me here.

The North Korean Embassy

Every day, Batkhuyak would take me from the Ministry of Environment and Tourism office back to the hotel, a walk of about two kilometers. Just around the corner from the ministry building was the North Korean Embassy. Near to the gate entrance were a number of plaques and photos displaying highlights of the leader Kim Jon Un and his reign. One day as I was walking back to the hotel with Batkhuyak, the gates to the embassy were open. There were no guards at the gate at the time. I thought it would be interesting to walk around inside the compound and be able to say that I had done that. However, after taking one step toward the gate, Batkhuyak grabbed my arm. He said cameras were watching, and being a Westerner, once inside that compound, they might not let me out so that was a bad idea. Apparently there are 1200 North Koreans who have work permits in Mongolia, and 100,000 who work abroad in the world.[2] Mongolia is one of only a few countries in the world that has a North Korean Embassy. The United Nations (UN) has a presence in Mongolia. I was told the UN facilitates communications through that North Korean Embassy, allowing many world nations to conduct business with them.

While in Mongolia, I also attended a briefing at the United Nations regarding MERIT projects. That was a first for me, attending a UN meeting.

The Energy Dilemma—Burning Coal for Heating the City

The energy used in Ulan Baatar comes from coal. During my first evening at the hotel, even though it was a cool evening, the heat coming from the old-style heat radiators was excessive, and even turning the knob to low did not seem to help. I went to sleep, and then woke up in the middle of the night sweating because the room was too hot. I decided to open the window and let some cooler air in. I went to sleep again, and as I woke up in the morning, the room was filled with the heavy stench of the smoke from the burning coal coming from outside, entering through my partially open window. Ulan Bataar is an extremely polluted city. As the days went by, I spent time traveling throughout some of the streets in Ulan Baatar. It was apparent that the energy infrastructure in this city is a problem. Central heating using coal and the large pipes to transmit the steam heat were substantial elements, quite ugly features in that urban landscape. Coal is the worst polluting fossil fuel source. I can attest through my experiences observing that coal energy production generates intolerable volumes of pollution and greenhouse gasses. There is certainly an opportunity for the advancement of energy management and clean energy development in Ulan Baatar.

Housing in Ulan Baatar

Ulan Baatar is a city of apartment dwellers, unlike the rural areas where many of the people still live in ger huts. In driving through the city, it seemed to me the greatest amount of construction was for new apartment complexes. There were older apartment buildings as well, of the Soviet-style, which were mass produced prior to the 1990s. Many of these complexes looked the same. There has been little attention paid to the aesthetic treatment of the buildings. Lands needed for central heating pipelines, many above the ground, were a land use planning and design nightmare as well. I noticed many of the newer style developments were high-rise buildings, constructed without too much imagination. Even in 2017, newer development projects were being replicated many times. There seemed to be a building boom happening during the time I was there, with buildings going up very quickly. Many of the aspects of city development in Ulan Baatar were very unique, and a higher level of city planning would be helpful.

Przewalski's Horses and Hustai National Park

I met Martinus (Martin) Housz and Michelle Karlzen, both MERIT technical advisors and both from Edmonton, Alberta. While in Ulan Bataar, and we spent a lot of our free time together, encountering some Indiana Jones adventures. We went to Hustai National Park to see the protected Przewalski's horses. These are like a miniature version of large Clydesdale horses I was familiar with in Canada. Przewalski's horses, as indicated in the tourist information at the hotel, are a rare and endangered horse native to the steppes of central Asia. They were taken to Poland and the Ukraine earlier in the twentieth century and became extinct in Mongolia. They have been reintroduced into the wild at Hustai National Park, and these efforts have been successful due to the aid of the International Union for Conservation of Nature (IUCN).

Lost in Mongolia

An experienced driver took us on the journey to Hustai Park, and we thought this driver was familiar with where we were going. We travelled about two hours west of Ulan Baatar, and from about forty-five minutes outside of Ulan Baatar, there was little traffic and little human population. We left the main highway, and there were only double-track dirt roads, and most in very rough condition. After entering the Hustai National Park, we drove a few hours more, but could not find the horses. We had travelled some distance on poor those roads, up high hills, and encountered snow. Then, we realized . . .we were lost! We asked the driver if he had been to the park before, and he revealed he had not. We all had assumed, that as our guide and driver, knew where we were going and that we would not get lost.

We Found the Przewalski's—But Where were We?

As we continued driving, it was difficult to see where the road was. Then, suddenly, we saw a bunch of those rare horses near us. Przewalski's are seldom seen, but we saw them. That was a thrill! However, after the excitement of observing the horses and taking pictures, we realized that we were still lost. The driver had a GPS, but it did not seem to work in this remote area, as no roads were recorded on it. Finally, after many kilometers of nothing, we found a Mongolian ger hut and thankfully, someone was living in it. Our driver spoke to a man in *Khalkha*, the main language of Mongolian, and was told that we had driven some distance outside of Hustai Park. He provided directions. Despite those extremely poor roads, and after another considerable drive, we were able to get back to the main gate. After that, there was no problem getting to the main highway, and then to Ulan Baatar. Wow, that was quite a day.

Gorkhi-Terelj National Park and the Genghis Khan Statue Complex

Martin, Michelle, and I also went to visit Gorkhi-Terelj National Park and the Genghis Khan Statue Complex, about a two-hour drive east of Ulan Baatar. The statue of Genghis will now be forever etched in my mind after having seen it—it was spectacular! We were driving on the main highway, fifty kilometers from the destination, when there was a bright glare ahead of us. The glare got brighter and brighter as we approached it. The closer we got, the more that image took shape; it was a stainless-steel statue of Genghis Khan on his horse, on top of an interpretive centre building. Built in 2008, it is the largest equestrian statue in the world. The main building is an interpretive centre featuring

Genghis Khan, the history of the Mongolian Empire, and an information and artifacts of Mongolian history and culture.

Ghenghis Khan—Now My Hero

On the return route to Ulan Baatar, beside the highway, there was an interesting photo opportunity for tourists. I was able to get some action pictures of myself pretending to be Genghis—I think I looked even more dynamic than Indiana Jones would have, in those pictures. I turned into a Mongolian warrior. I mingled with giant vultures and camels from the Mongolian Gobi Desert—this was my Mongolian safari.

Martin, Michelle, and I went on a hike at Gorkhi-Terelj National Park, close to Ulan Baatar and we got a feel for the vast openness of Mongolia. We also toured some ger huts. At intervals along the roads, there were alters for Buddhist worshipping, and we stopped at one. The Buddhists go around the alters three times and bow to Buddha in respect. I did that, hoping the spirit of Buddha would stay with me. This was a very, very nice day. A part of Genghis Khan will always be in my thoughts, I am sure.

Mongolian Wrestling

To fully appreciate Mongolia, you must see a Mongolian wrestling competition—Martin and I went to the coliseum in Ulan Baatar. It was an all-afternoon event on a Sunday. I love sports, almost any sport. The sport of wrestling is a huge part of Mongolian culture, like what hockey is in Canada. The Mongolians are immensely proud of their wrestlers. Martin and I took a taxi to the venue and had ringside seats. The event took a long time to begin. There were a lot of speeches, a Buddhist ceremony, a lot of meditating and chanting, introductions of competitors, and finally the wrestling events.

There were 106 wrestlers competing to be the champion on that day. There were up to eight matches taking place at one time on the inner floor. The wrestlers were exceptionally large and muscular. You do not want to make those guys angry! The officials for each match were Buddhist monks, and prior to fighting, each wrestler had to circle the monk three times going clockwise, receive a blessing, and then be ready for the match. A wrestler putting his opponent to the floor was the winner, and he received a ribbon which was placed on the back of his hat. There was an altar in the corner of the coliseum floor, where the winner of the match was blessed by another monk at that altar. Things kept moving along for several hours, and it was hard to keep track of everything. We left before the event concluded and an ultimate winner was declared. It was getting late, and we had been there for the entire afternoon. I had enjoyed that afternoon.

Bring Home a Horse Fiddle—Morin Khuur

My trip home was also interesting. My son Lance, back in Canada, is a musician in his spare time. He asked me to bring him a horsehead fiddle, which in Mongolia is called a morin khuur. You play it like a violin, but the music is totally different. The top end hand has an ornamental horse-head shape, and the other end is like an odd-angled box. My son Lance occasionally uses this horsehead fiddle for some of his musical gigs on Vancouver Island, Canada, where he lives.

Lance was lucky to get this instrument because transporting it back to Canada, including a check-in, security checks, and customs was a hassle at every turn. It was too long for carry-on, I was searched for suspicious material, and there was a dispute about whether the duty allowance was exceeded. The instrument was also fragile, too large for compartments, and had to be handled carefully. Persistence and smooth talking got this item home safely, undamaged, and with no customs duty or oversize charge. Mission accomplished and a major challenge was overcome.

Mining Can Be Controversial

I did not know that Canada is such a huge global player in mining. Mongolia has determined that it will pursue resource development and mining to allow it to prosper as a country. But no matter where you are, mining will always come with some level of controversy, and I saw evidence of opposition on street posters in Ulan Baatar. I was not aware how widespread that opposition was. I was told that Rio Tinto was a multi-national company connected to Canada, Australia, England, and the USA, and it was being criticized in those outdoor public posters. Also under criticism were the local "ninja miners," the small operators who extract resources without approvals and usually without regard to proper environmental protection practices. Ninja miners do their business in the black market and it is hard to detect their unlawful activities. It has been a challenge for the Mongolian enforcement officers to catch them.

Canada is attempting to help Mongolia find a balance between the economic benefits from mining and management of the environment. I was a small part of that effort through the MERIT program, and I hope this balance can be achieved.

Mongolia in the Rear View Mirrow

Mongolian culture is unique. The transition of this country from communism to a free-market economy has produced a sort of hybrid nation of sorts. Although located between China and Russia, it retains a unique and distinct culture. This, to me is quite remarkable. I will never forget the stunning and amazing Genghis Khan statues, commonplace throughout the country. I do not want to get lost in Mongolia again, because outside of Ulan Bataar, people are few and far between. If the GPS does not work, it could be goodbye! The wrestling . . . cashmere . . . interesting people—what an exciting time that was! Everyone should go to Mongolia at least once.

FOOTNOTES

1. Mongolia National Census 2017 Results, National Statistical Office of Mongolia, as cited in Wikipedia

2. Agence France Presse, December 2017; translation cited in Wikipedia

CESO Work, the Ulan Bataar Scene, and Pollution

From top left: MERIT Advisors Martin Houz, Michelle Karlzen and myself; Mongolian Government complex; Batkhuyak Naigal and myself; Environment legal staff, translator, and myself; Inspection Agency meeting for MERIT assignment; United Nations Building in Ulan Baatar; Gated North Korean Embassy – Ulan Baatar; Mongolian landscape; Panoramic view of Ulan Baatar; Dinner with Canadian MERIT advisors in Mongolia; Traditional Mongolian Clothing; A typical Buddhist altar along many roadsides

Ghenghis Khan Statue, Prezynski's Horses, Mongolian Wrestling, and the Morin Khur

From top left: Horsemeat and cabbage; Attractive boulevard and sidewalk spaces; Chaotic parking in random spaces between building; Morin Khuur; Horse head grip on end of Morin Khuur; Coal energy plant; Above ground pipes – thermal heating using coal; Coal-fired plant air pollution; Dirt Road to Hustai National Park; Hustai National Park – looking for Przewalski horses; Lost in the Mongolian wilderness; We found the Przewalski horses

From top left: The Ghenghis Khan monument – Gorghi Trelji National Park; Gorghi Trelji National Park entry; My photo opp in Mongolian Warrior gear; A Mongolian warrior statue; Home for most people in Ulan Baatar; My photo opp with a Mongolian vulture; Unique Mongolian architecture; Ger styled homes prevalent throughout Mongolia; Mongolian wrestlers before the fight; Several wrestling matches at the same time; Competitors circling the Buddhist alter before the match; Award presentation – wrestling

Chapter 12

CHINA

Exploring Hong Kong and Beijing in 2013 and 2017

Map produced by Lance Smith

About China

The Socialist Republic of China has the largest population of any country in the world with about 1.5 billion people. The two cities I visited were Beijing and Hong Kong. Beijing has a population of 20.5 million and Hong Kong has a population of 7.5 million. [1] China has a long, well documented, and fascinating history. Important for the context of my visits, Hong Kong was formerly a British colony, and it was transferred back to the Republic in 1997. China itself is under authoritarian communist rule, but the transfer of Hong Kong came with a proviso that Hong Kong would continue to operate democratically under a separate special status constitution. It is now 2021, and I have not been to Beijing or Hong Kong for a few years. It looks like the freedom which Hong Kong has enjoyed for decades will be disappearing.

Beijing is the capital of the People's Republic of China. It is the world's most populous national capital with over 21 million people. [2] Beijing is the nation's political and cultural center and a powerful economic force in the country. There was much to see in Beijing including the ancient historical and cultural destinations as well as more modern edifices.

Speaking very frankly from the events recent, I am appalled at the barbaric behaviour of the Republic of China, its treatment of Hong Kong, and its bullying nature in doing business around the world. Looking back at my visits and the exposure to Hong Kong and Beijing, perhaps there were already some hints of that during my time visiting those cities in China.

The Hong Kong Experience

After the completion of my assignment in the Philippines in late 2012, our family scheduled a five-day stopover in Hong Kong, arriving on January 1, 2013, before returning home. There were wonderful things to see in Hong Kong. A significant percentage of the population spoke English and generally all were kind and helpful, once they were engaged in a conversation.

Upon arrival in Hong Kong, you realize the density of population is extreme. Huge high-rise buildings, and lots of people! Our first adventure while there was to go to Victoria Park, and then up a mountain on a rail cable tram car, where the entire city of Hong Kong could be viewed. The line-up was incredibly long, but it was moving efficiently. The tram route was very steep, a bit scary, but you just "hung-on tight" - it was fine.

The skyline of Hong Kong is really something to see. There are not too many small buildings, mostly huge ones surrounding the coastline. Construction was taking place throughout the city, and cranes were apparent throughout the skyline to accommodate the continuation of more and more high-rise buildings. In 2013, Hong Kong was growing rapidly, and mostly vertically.

Transportation in Hong Kong

Getting around Hong Kong is not as bad as in some other major cities, for several reasons. These include staggered work hours, strict travel timing restrictions, high parking fees for the mostly underground parking, expensive taxis, and because it has the best mass transit and subway system in the world. The transit system is efficient, comfortable, fast, and easy to use. So, who needs a car in Hong Kong? Thanks to an excellent transportation system, life without a vehicle in Hong Kong is not so bad. It is so easy to get around. That is surprising for a city of more than seven million people.

We took the transit system a few times, enroute to seeing Lantau Island and Ocean Park. Boat transportation, such as the Star Ferry, is another important transportation option for this ocean city with the many water crossings between Kowloon and the main part of Hong Kong.

Buying a Custom Tailored Suit and Jewelry

While walking around the Kowloon area near our hotel, a man of East-Indian descent kept confronting me on the street. He was a tailor, and he kept asking me to come to his shop. He wanted to make me a silk suit. He kept after me for three days, until on the last day in Hong Kong, I finally agreed. I went to his small shop and he had me pick out the material. He took a lot of care and attention into taking my exact measurements. Unfortunately, the suit was not ready by our departure time, so it was sent by mail to Canada. It cost about $200 in Canadian currency. A few days after returning home, the suit arrived in the mail. It was not a scam! It fit perfectly. It is the best suit I have ever had, and it is only worn on special occasions.

Hong Kong is also famous for making some of the finest jewelry in the world. Our family toured the famous Dynasty Jewelry facility and wholesale store. A ring and necklace were purchased for Clarita, since during our 2003 wedding in Canada, we did not have an appropriate ring, so this was how we made up for it.

Ocean Park

One of the days in Hong Kong, we went to Ocean Park, a ninety-two-hectare marine and animal theme park. There was a wide range of things do there including an amusement park. Of course, the aquarium and seeing live pandas and riding in a rickshaw were special experiences. This was a fun time for our family.

Lantu Island and the Tian Tan Buddha Statue

We also spent a day going to Lantau Island to see the Tian Tan Buddha Statue, a major tourist attraction. As well as taking the subway to get to the island, we went on a long gondola ride across the water to get there. The bottom of the gondola was glass, and I refused to look at the floor, as we were high up, and it was a long way down to the ground. The kids had no fear, and they enjoyed viewing the ground below their feet without any hesitation. Once we got off the gondola, it was a lengthy walk to get to the statue, and there were a lot of stairs to climb to get up to it. But the walk was worth it to see the enormous Tian Tan statute, of such cultural significance. There were also many other remarkably interesting Buddha related statues to see near the main attraction, the Tian Tan Buddha statue.

The Temple Night Market

On the final evening before leaving Hong Kong, Clarita and I went to the Temple Street Night Market. It was an incredibly busy place. Anything you needed to purchase; you could find it there. I was told to be careful about pickpockets, so I was extra cautious protecting my wallet. Although it was a crowded place, there were no problems. However, the precautions taken may have slowed down our shopping experience. At the end of a few hours, not much of anything was purchased, but at least we got to see one of the most interesting night markets anywhere. We found a taxi to take us back to the hotel, and the next day, we flew back to Canada.

The Beijing Experience

In October 2017, travelling to and from the MERIT assignment in Ulan Baatar, Mongolia, involved layovers in Beijing. People say first impressions are significant, and that may be true about my first impressions of Beijing. I had an eerie feeling the whole time I was there. Enroute to Mongolia on October first, the aircraft arrived at about one p.m. It was Chinese National Day, commemorating the founding of the People's Republic of China in 1949. The airport was extremely crowded, more packed than any airport I had ever been in. A huge airport with people jammed together like sardines and in long line-ups with police and military personnel everywhere. To enter China, one needs either a work visa, which is a thirty-day visitor visa, or a seventy-two-hour short-stay visa. I needed to get the seventy-two-hour visa for a twenty-seven-hour layover at an airport hotel before taking the connecting flight. It took me the rest of the day just to get out of that airport. Nobody spoke English, except for non-citizens, and nobody was being too friendly or wanting to answer questions.

Getting Through the Airport—Customs, Security, and Visitor Visa

There was a lengthy process to go through the required formalities at the airport.

First step, exit the plane.

Second step, find the visa wicket and get a seventy-two-hour short stay visa. It was a wait of over three hours. This would have been very painful were it not for an Australian and a Swiss traveler next to me. They were both joke tellers, and we had some interesting conversations.

Third step, customs check and a one hour wait.

Fourth step, security check and another one hour wait.

Fifth step, a ten-minute walk to a shuttle train, to another terminal building to retrieve my baggage. The train ride was fast, it only took another ten minutes. This was efficient.

Sixth step, go to the carousel and retrieve baggage. There was no baggage on the carousels because it was almost six hours after the arrival of that plane. I tried to find my baggage, but nobody spoke English or seemed very willing to help me out. Finally, a Filipino couple who were also travelling walked past me, and they were also looking for their baggage. They spoke English and let me tag along with them, and they helped me. The Filipino word for thank you in Tagalog is "salamat." We were finally able to locate the compound at the end of the carousels where the luggage was, and the Filipino folks and I retrieved our bags.

The final step was to exit the baggage terminal and find the shuttle service to the Beijing Holiday Inn. It was dark outside by this time, and the lighting was poor. Everyone who was around that terminal area was too busy to answer my questions and I do not believe anybody there spoke English. I could not find my shuttle service. There must have been over 200 station points for shuttle services. Finally, a security guard did give me directions. I asked him where the Holiday Inn transfer shuttle was. He pointed his finger to a direction and I walked past four or five station points, and there was the hotel sign for that shuttle. After a short wait, I was on my way and got to the hotel safely.

That was not a fun day! I was exhausted after all that.

The next day, I travelled to Ulan Bataar on a China Air flight. On return to Beijing from Ulan Baatar, I was able to check-in and get through the airport process with less difficulty, but there was never a smile on my face while I was at that airport.

Touring Beijing in 2017

On my return trip to Canada from Mongolia, I had a day-long layover in Beijing. I decided to book a tour online with a guide by the name of Alexandra Lieu. She turned out to be a particularly good guide, and she showed me a lot of things in the city. It was October 10, 2017, and this time I was able to exit the airport in only two and a half hours. I was supposed to look for Alexandra, holding a card with my name on it. When I exited the airport baggage terminal, there was an area for pick-up, and there were hundreds of people behind a roped-off area, many holding cards with names. I walked up and down the roped area looking for the card with my name on it, but I did not see it. I must have done that circuit three times and nothing. This did not feel good . . . what would I do if Alexandra did not show up? Finally, I saw a man holding a card that read "David Smith—Canada." I said to him, "Hello, that is my name, but you are not Alexandra?" The man said in broken English, "Alexandra gone washroom, no worries, she come soon." The panic attack was over.

Tiananmen Square and Significant Buildings

I met Alexandra and we found Alexandra's driver. They took me to the infamous central downtown of Beijing. We were dropped off near Tiananmen Square, near the end of daylight. We watched the renowned daily ceremony - taking down the flag. The flag of China is raised every in the morning and is taken down at sunset. There were many soldiers and security guards on hand, and a huge crowd watching the flag coming down. There was a barrier fence ensuring that nobody could get too close to the marching soldiers or the flag. After the ceremony, you cannot enter Tiananmen Square or any of the buildings or the adjacent Forbidden City. Alexandra told me that within the square are the Monument to the People's Heroes, the Great Hall of the People, the National Museum of China, and the Mausoleum of Mao Zedong. She explained that Mao Zedong proclaimed the founding of the People's Republic of China in the square on October 1, 1949, and the anniversary of this event was still observed there.

Tiananmen Square is one of the ten largest city squares in the world containing forty-four hectares or 109 acres.[3] it has great cultural significance, as it was the site of several important events in Chinese history. Outside China, the square is best known for the 1989 Tiananmen Square protests that ended with a military crackdown, and the infamous Tiananmen Square Massacre. Watching those marching soldiers was certainly an eerie feeling, knowing the history of that place. Because of the time of day, the area was gated and guarded, and I did not get to see inside the Forbidden City, but I was able to skirt around the edges of it. The night lighting around the wall was quite majestic. I learned that inside was the Imperial Palace, which dated back as far as the Ming Dynasty of the fourteenth century. My choice for the short time that I was in Beijing, was to either go to the Forbidden Palace or the Great Wall. I would have loved to see them both, but I chose the Great Wall.

Crazy Street - Wangfujing Snack Street

Alexandra outlined some things to see in the evening to maximize my time during the short layover. She set a fast pace for the tight evening schedule. A few blocks walk from the square was "Crazy Street," or the Wangfujing Snack Street. This area was truly bizarre. There were snack outlets with foods most foreigners would have never seen before. There were live scorpions on a stick, and cooked foods such as centipede, snake, starfish, silkworm, seahorse, cockroaches, grasshoppers, slugs, cow's stomach, sheep's penis, some unique beverages, and more. One might think this food would be a turn off, but that was not the case. This area of Beijing was extremely crowded, and that food was in demand.

The Hutong Area

Alexandra had another plan for dinner, and she took me to a *hutong* area. Hutong is a narrow lane, alley, or small street between rows of single-storey traditional Chinese dwellings (*Siheyuans*). This area was a big contrast from the glitz of the bright lights of the inner-city commercial area. She said the real culture of Beijing is in the culture of Hutong and Siheyuan, which represented the historical lifestyle of ordinary *Beijingers*. We walked down a dark narrow alley until we found what looked like a garage with a sign and Chinese décor, a quite simple place. It was a restaurant accessed from a garage-like building in a laneway. The meal was tremendous, cooked to perfection in the Chinese way.

Cultural Street and Bar Street

After dinner, the fast-paced evening continued. We saw Cultural Street, a pedestrian only roadway containing some nice museums, shops, and galleries. It was connected to Bar Street, also a pedestrian only street. In the middle of the street was a creek, and on both sides, there were pedestrian walking areas with dozens of small bars and restaurants, most of them having live bands. It was a Tuesday evening, but there were a lot of people enjoying themselves. Because it was later in the evening, I was unable to take pictures.

Olympic Facilities—the Bird's Nest and the Cube

The last event for the evening was to do a drive-by of the main facilities for the 2008 Olympics. We could not enter the buildings because they were closed at that time. First, there was the Bird's Nest. I was told the stadium had a capacity of 91,000 seats, in its design for the main Olympic events such as track and field and the opening and closing ceremonies. Next, we viewed the Cube with several pools under one roof. The facility was used for the Olympic swimming and diving events.

It was after eleven p.m. when we departed from these impressive facilities. It was very dark, and seeing these buildings lit-up was impressive. As with the Forbidden Palace and the Monument to the People's Heroes, these were only viewed from a distance. If I go to Beijing again, I will try to gain access to go inside them or at least see them close-up.

That was one exhausting evening. Alexandra booked me into the JI Hotel in Dongzhimen Beijing, near downtown, and not too far from those Olympic facilities. It was a small, modest hotel with a bed, television, and shower, and not much more than that. But that was fine. I got to the hotel at midnight and had to wake up at five a.m. for breakfast, checkout, and a pick-up to see the Great Wall of China before the departing flight for Canada in the early after-noon. I did not see other foreigners at this hotel, and nobody spoke or under-stood much English. It was always an adventure to communicate in Beijing, even for simple things. I was happy when Alexandra and the driver arrived that morning. In mainland China, you should have an interpreter and Alexandra, the tour guide, could speak English quite well. Without her interpreting, the tour could have been a disaster.

The Great Wall of China—the Mutianyu Great Wall Section

It took a couple of hours to drive to the Mutianyu Great Wall located in the Huairou District of Beijing, twenty kilometers past the Jingcheng freeway. I was advised that this section of the Great Wall was the best one to see because it has been diligently preserved and restored better than the other wall sections, even though those attractions were a bit closer to the City of Beijing. The Mutianyu section, I was told, also contains the most scenic views of the nearby mountains.

I had a passion to see the Great Wall since 1988, when I was the planning director of Moose Jaw, Saskatchewan. At the time, a Chinese delegation visited the city for a trade mission, part of the opening-up of trade between China and the free world, prior to the eminent transfer of the governance of Hong Kong by the British to the People's Republic of China. The 1980s was part of the shift toward China becoming part of the global community. Those Chinese delegates, at a banquet, presented all the Moose Jaw city officials, including me, with a beautiful tapestry of the Great Wall. This has always hung on my living room wall, and it is a prized possession. A future visit to the Great Wall of China was always on my bucket list.

The Great Wall . . . it is difficult to find words to describe it. On arrival, you need to take a cable car from the entry point up to the Great Wall itself. The cable ride took about ten minutes, and then I found myself "frozen in the moment." A surge of adrenaline hit me. I was on the Wall! I was walking on the wall for less than five minutes when my cell phone rang. To my surprise, it was my oldest daughter Terra from Campbell River, Canada. I had been trying to contact her, and other family in Canada, for over a week, without success. She had also been trying to contact me as well. For this call to happen when it did, was special. I tried in my own words to share the moment with her, and pictures were texted. I should have said, "one giant step for this man." That was a beautiful moment for me to share with Terra and my grandson Logan who was with her. I will not forget that.

Alexandra had an injured leg that day, so she stayed near the cable car area.

She told me to navigate the wall by myself, which I did for about two hours. It was not crowded that day and there were tourists from all over the world speaking many different languages. The Great Wall, as everyone who has been there will tell you, is an impressive human accomplishment. This is a formidable, solid structure, and I see how it would have kept the Mongols from invading China. There were lots and lots of stairs to climb, up and down. It was a bit exhausting, but a magical day.

It was a bit sad to depart from the Great Wall. While I was at the exit area to go back down, I had a choice. I could either take the chairlift down or go on a lengthy slide ride, which would take me right down the mountain to a point near to the entry gate. I decided to again take the cable car with Alexandra. Virtually nobody was taking the slide that morning, although it might have been more in keeping with an Indiana Jones adventure. At the bottom of the hill were souvenir shops and lots of security guards. I asked one of the guards if I could have a picture taken with him. I anticipated he would say no, because in China, you do not question the military. They tend to make you uncomfortable by their presence. However, it was a good day, and he agreed to have the picture taken.

Time to Go Home

The traffic back to the airport was manageable. I was told the freeway can get congested, but around noon on October 11, it was fine. The visit was an early morning one. It had to be done efficiently. The airport check-in at the Air Canada and security checks went smoothly for the afternoon flight home to Canada.

I am thankful to have Alexandra and the driver for the fantastic Beijing tour and getting me around Beijing over a two-day period, promptly and safely. Despite tight timelines, there was little or no stress. That fast-paced tour I will never forget. Scratch the Great Wall from my bucket list.

China in the Rear View Mirror

I have some conclusions on my brief travels within China. There are things to see there that you will not see anywhere else. The interesting cultural and historical artifacts you see in China are things that will not be forgotten. Seeing Hong Kong and Beijing was special.

I am troubled by recent events involving China. These events have really dampened my desire to ever return there. As most Canadians are well aware, in 2018, Meng Wenzhou, a senior executive and chief financial officer of Huawei, China's largest privately held company and telecom giant, was arrested in Canada. This was on a provisional U.S. extradition request in regard to the alleged defrauding of multiple financial institutions in breach of U.S. sanctions against Iran.[2] This was a serious offence and the rule of law had to be applied. In response to this arrest, two Canadians working in China, Michael Kovrig and Michael Spavor were thrown in jail in China. There seems to be little doubt these allegations against the two Canadians were unfounded and they were fabricated by China as a blunt retaliation against the possible extradition of Meng Wenzhou. Meng is now back in China and the two Michaels are free and are back in Canada. That may be good, but I suspect the relations between Canada and China will not be very good for many years into the future.

Hong Kong's protests started in June 2019, voicing opposition to the Fugitive Offenders Amendment bill in Hong Kong, which would permit extradition to mainland China. Many in Hong Kong feared this could undermine the current judicial independence of Hong Kong and endanger dissidents. It would end the special status democracy in place in Hong Kong and mean the loss of longstanding freedoms prior to the deadline.

In reflecting on my travels to China in 2013 and 2017, China was not as comfortable a place to travel as other countries. It is a dictatorship. Hong Kong as of mid-2020 still has special status as a democracy, so it is supposed to have a lot of freedoms. In 2012, it did not feel so much like a country under the rule of a communist dictatorship. But the times have changed.

In 2017 in Beijing, I did not feel very relaxed while there. Nobody was too friendly, except for my tour guide Alexandra and her driver. It seemed as if everyone wanted to be careful and not get into trouble. People do not want to talk to or be seen talking to foreigners. At least, that is what I saw. I was happy to get through all the security checks, customs, and all other areas of clearance.

I was happy to get onto the Air Canada plane and land in Canada. As for the future of China, they are not team-players with the rest of the world. I have no desire to return to that country. I say to China . . . bring freedom and self-esteem to all Chinese people and "keep your hands off" Hong Kong.

FOOTNOTES

1. <u>National Bureau of Statistics of China</u>, November 1, 2010; as cited in Wikipedia
2. <u>Global News</u>; June 27, 2019; as cited in Wikipedia
3. <u>Tiananmen Square</u>, 2007, Britannica Concise Encyclopedia as cited in Wikipedia

Pictures of the Hong Kong Visit

From top left: Panoramic view – Hong Kong skyline from Victoria Park; Crane and a Construction boom in Hong Kong – 2013; Family picture at Ocean Park; Ocean Park (amusement, zoo, aquarium); Panda at the Ocean Park Zoo; Taxi service by boat to Ocean Park; A Chinese rickshaw; The famous Tian Tan Statue at Lantau Island; More Buddha Statues; Glass floor of the Langtu Island Gondola; Custom tailored silk suit; Hong Kong Dynasty Jewelry Factory

Pictures of the Beijing Visit

From top left: Congested Beijing Airport – National holiday – October 1, 2017; Great Hall of the People Congress; Peripheral Area of Tianamen Square; Looking towards Tianamen Square; Another view – Tianamen Square; National Museum of China – across from Tianamen Square; The walls outside the Forbidden City at night; Traditional Chinese attire; Hutong area; Wangfujing Snack Street (Crazy Street); Birds Nest olympic facility; Cube Olympic Facility
<Pictures of the Hutong area and Olympic Facilities – the Birds Nest and the Cube are courtesy of Creative Commons Free Stock Photos

Pictures at the Great Wall of China

From top left: Daughter Terra and my Grandson Logan – called me as I stepped onto The Great Wall; Guard at The Great Wall of China; The Great Wall of China; The Great Wall of China; The Great Wall of China; The Great Wall of China; The Great Wall of China; The Great Wall of China; The Great Wall of China; The Great Wall of China; The Great Wall of China; The Great Wall of China

Chapter 13

SURINAME AND JAMAICA

Assignments in Two Countries of the Caribbean World
and Explorations While There in
Suriname 2017 and Jamaica in 2019

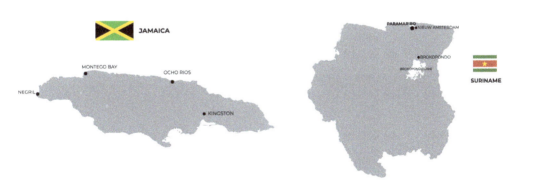

Map produced by Lance Smith

About Suriname

Suriname is located north of Brazil, in between the countries of Guyana and French Guyana in South America. It is a coastal country fronting the Atlantic Ocean next to the Caribbean Sea. It is a member of CARICOM, the Caribbean Group of Communities. It is more often referenced as being part of the Caribbean as opposed to being part of South America due to closer ties to that part of the world. It contains a population of about 570,000 residents. [1] It was a colony of the Netherlands dating back to the 1600s but received independence in 1975. Like Canada, it contains a multi-cultural, ethnic mix. The official language spoken is Dutch, but Surinamese Creole (Surinamese Tongo) in day-to-day life, is more widely used. Suriname consists of Indians (from India), descendants of enslaved Africans, and Javanese as the largest groups, there are also Europeans (mostly Dutch), Amerindians, Chinese, Jewish, and some other groups residing in Suriname. [2]

The economy of Suriname has struggled in recent years. The country is dependent on resources, primarily oil and gold, and unfortunately, the price for these commodities has been weak the past few years. What was once the largest employer, the Alcan Aluminum Plant, closed in 2017. This closure had a devastating impact on the economy of hat country. The mining of bauxite, which is used in aluminum production continues, but exporting has not been consistent. At the time I was there, Suriname had the third highest rate of inflation in the world, behind Venezuela and South Sudan. [3]

Travelling to Suriname

I was picked up at the Paramaribo airport on March 1, 2018, by Fulgor Esajas, manager at Stichting Vonzell. The flight was late arriving, and it took a long time to clear customs and purchase a visa. My plane arrived at this small airport at the same time as a KLM Boeing 747 from Amsterdam, resulting in lengthy line-ups. A driver who was picking me up was also waiting for another passenger, and I had to wait about another hour for that passenger to be located. When we eventually got to the hotel downtown it was after midnight, and the cast iron gates in front were locked, and there was nobody there to let us in. The driver then dropped off the other passenger at a different hotel nearby. After that, Fulgor searched for another accommodation for me. We finally found a suitable guest house, modest, but fine.

The trip to Suriname was long and exhausting. The route was Kelowna, Calgary, Toronto, Port of Spain (Trinidad Tobago), and finally to Parimaribo, Suriname. There were different airlines - Air Canada, Caribbean Airways, and Suriname Air taking me to Suriname. There were delays and a long layover in Port of Spain, and fortunately a hotel was provided for me to have a rest during the lengthy wait for that connection.

The CESO Assignment

I was accepted to do a CESO assignment based in Parimaribo, the capital city of Suriname in 2018. The assignment was to complete a strategic business plan including capacity building for the Stichting Vonzell Foundation. This umbrella organization assists other non-profit social service agencies in areas of youth employment, individuals living with disabilities, HIV/Aids support, gender equality, employment training in perma-culture, and sport development.

The first order of business was to have an introductory meeting with the client. Present were Leander Zeldenrust, owner and operator of Stichting Vonzell, Fulgar Esajas, chief assistant at Vonzell, Sheila Ketwaru, country representative for CESO, and me.

After discussions with the client, it became apparent that the other stakeholder organizations also wanted help with establishing or updating their strategic plans. But there was more. It was determined by Vonzell that their primary need was to find foreign donor money to assist with their proposed programming and projects. They requested my assistance in completing funding applications and developing a strategy to secure greater funding. Meetings were held with the Vonzell staff, and the stakeholders and the tasks were completed. However, the client was hoping for a fast-track to international fundraising. I did my best to help, but they wanted guaranteed, secure funding to sustain their well-intended efforts, but it just could not be done as a direct outcome of this project.

A Permaculture Project for employing Youth

Leander was very enthusiastic about her initiative to develop a project which would achieve multiple objectives. She took me for a drive to show me her project. It involved several hectares of land about an hour out of Paramaribo owned by Vonzell. The plan was to develop the land for permaculture (a form of organic agriculture). This was proposed to be an environmentally sensitive operation without the use of chemicals or spraying. The site would involve the training of youth for employment in agriculture, and jobs would be created. I was quite impressed with the concept. However, upon arriving to view this site in a rainforest area (part of the amazon basin) in Suriname, I viewed work in progress. The area was clear-cut rainforest, with numerous ponds, logs, and debris pilings throughout the site. I do not think the pros and cons of this project had been fully evaluated or given an environmental assessment, although the project was well-intended.

While in the Vonzell office, I helped them to prepare documentation for their applications for donor funding. I am not sure if this helped them in their mission or not, but I tried to assist them.

CESO Presentation to the Paramaibo Chamber of Commerce

Sheila Ketwaru, the Country Representative for CESO in Suriname also asked me to attend a Chamber of Commerce meeting with her in Paramaribo a day before I was to return to Canada. The purpose was to explain the role of CESO in aiding developing countries. She wanted to see if there was any interest from those businesses and organizations attending, in initiating future assignments. The meeting was informative, and the snacks and pastries were excellent. I am not sure if this helped generate interest or any future CESO assignments, but it was nice to meet many interesting people that evening. After the meeting, Sheila took me for some Indonesian Soto Soup, a first for me. It was good. I think Anthony Bourdain would have enjoyed that soup.

Holi and the Phagwa Festival

Have you ever been to a place where people celebrate by throwing powder or liquid colours on each other? Well, Fulgar Esajas took me to the Phagwa Festival for a few hours, where they do just that. Many people wore white clothes to dramatize the colour effect. The Phagwa Festival, meaning "the festival of colour," is part of Holi, a national holiday in Suriname. It is celebrated to mark the beginning of spring, and it originates in Hindu mythology. This is a wild and crazy party, where everyone is happy and joyful. I tried to be a bystander, but I got splashed with the coloured chalk as well.

Touring Historic Forts—Zeelandia and Nieuw Amsterdam

I was able to fit a couple of tours into the time schedule. There are two forts strategically located along the Suriname River, and I was able to tour both. Fort Zeelandia is located adjacent to downtown Paramaribo. It had interpretive displays depicting the nation's history and colonization by the Netherlands, the history of slavery, and the development of the town of Paramaribo. Areas in the Caribbean were a battleground for colonization, so much of the displays featured military equipment.

Fort Nieuw Amsterdam is located further inland about twenty-five kilometers from Fort Zeelander, at the junction of the Suriname and Commewijne rivers. It is now a mostly open-air museum. It was necessary for the Dutch to construct this fortress to protect the territory from colonial invasions, particularly from the British and the French. In more recent years and until 1967, the fort was used as a prison.

Plantage Frederiksdorp

Near to Nieuw Amsterdam was Plantage Frederiksdorp, located downstream about thirty kilometers from Paramaribo. We had to drive most of the distance and then park the vehicle. We took a boat across the river and then docked at this plantation site, which is now a museum. At Plantage Frederiksdorp, there is lodging for tourists, who can experience a relaxing, quiet getaway. I only stayed there a few hours. This was once a coffee and cacao plantation in the eighteenth century, run by the Dutch, using slave labour. The buildings were all well preserved in the traditional Dutch architecture of the time. This plantation compound was attractively landscaped and well maintained.

The Dolphin Sunset Tour, the Johan, and Margaretha Plantation

On the weekend while in Parimaribo, I went on the Dolphin sunset tour. The guide navigated our boat a short distance into the Atlantic Ocean. The boat was old and slow, with peeling paint, but it transported us on schedule without problems. The tourists from the Netherlands were speaking Dutch, and others on board were from Sweden, also not speaking much English. The boat crew did not speak English either, so I just used hand signals in combination with simple English words for the communications. Everyone on that tour seemed to enjoy the natural surroundings. We saw some dolphins in the distance, but they were very illusive, and we could not seem to catch up with them. The ride was lengthy, but the unique scenery was interesting. We went down part of the Suriname River to the former plantation of Johan and Margaretha. It was no longer a plantation, but now a small village with a sawmill at the edge of the settlement. There was a dinner provided at a small restaurant, with a nice terrace overlooking the river. The mosquitoes were quite bad. I used up a lot of repellent, just as I had done many years ago growing up in Manitoba, Canada. This tour usually featured a picturesque sunset, but due to the cloudy weather and some rain, it was not ideal conditions for that. However, it was a good day, without Indiana Jones surprises. Sometimes it is nice to just kick-back and enjoy the surroundings of a new, interesting place.

The Neveh Shalom Jewish Synagogue and the Keizerstraat Mosque

I did observe something incredibly special in Paramaribo. I was shown two places of worship - Muslim and Jewish. They were situated side-by-side. Anywhere else in the world, this would not likely happen as these religious groups are usually in conflict with each other. The Neveh Shalom Jewish

Synagogue and the Keizerstraat Mosque were well-maintained religious build-ings. This was upheld as a highlight tourism destination, and all visitors are encouraged to see this. I was told that Suriname revels in its cultural diversity. That country is extremely tolerant of racial or religious differences. I was told that the central recreation building between the synagogue and the mosque are shared and scheduled cooperatively between both the Jewish and the Muslim groups. Not an Indiana Jones conflict to deal with here, peaceful and stress free in this situation.

A CT Scan

While in Paramaribo, I did encounter some digestive issues, and I was having some abdominal pain. In Canada, I had been diagnosed with fatty liver disease, and I was told to watch my diet. When travelling, that is not always so easy to do. After seeking some advice, I was told it might be a good idea to get a CT scan to determine if my condition was any worse than my testing from several years ago in Canada. There was a private diagnostic clinic in Paramaribo, run by a Dutch medical firm, and it was very reputable.

I went to the clinic and had the scan done. This might have cost several thousand dollars in Canada, but it was about $320 (Canadian) once the money was converted. I was pleased that my travel medical insurance covered that cost after my return home. The physician confirmed that I had lesions on my liver consistent with fatty liver disease, and that I should maintain a very low-fat and low-carbohydrate diet, to avoid further problems. I always keep trying to do that. It was comforting to know that the liver condition had not worsened in the past few years.

Trinidad Tobago and Aruba

On route to Suriname, I had a layover in Trinidad Tobago, two main islands and a population of 1.4 million. [3] The departure on Suriname Airlines was delayed, so I was able to talk to some others at the airport. Trinidad Tobago is a former British colony, so most speak English very well. I ate lunch outside the airport with a happy local guy. He loved his country, and he had a lot of jokes to tell.

On my return to Canada, the route included travelling through Aruba, a beautiful Caribbean island. I again had to switch planes and there was a lengthy delay. It was supposed to be a short stop-over, but the Air Canada aircraft encountered a mechanical delay of six hours. Travelling can be very exhausting.

Aruba is a popular tourist destination. It has a resident population of about 107,000 people. Aruba is a constituent country of the Republic of the Netherlands. The main languages are Dutch and Papiamento, an African Creole dialect. [4] I only saw Aruba from the air and from the airport, but it was a beautiful place from what I could see. I met a young couple from Toronto who go to Aruba every year. They said it is the best place in the world. At the airport, there were interesting souvenir shops and a popular, locally made pistachio liquor, which I tasted, and it was good. That was something special to buy from Aruba. I brought a bottle back for my wife Clarita, and it did not last long.

Suriname in the Rear View Mirror

Suriname was an interesting place to visit. It is a beautiful tropical country. I observed a deep sense of frustration in the eyes of the people, regarding their future. Although the people are friendly and they love their country, there seemed to be a sense of hopelessness in their general attitudes, as the economy was a mess in 2018. I hope Suriname finds a way to a brighter future.

Pictures of Parimaribo and Areas in Suriname

From top left: CESO start-up meeting – Stichting Vonzell and Suriname CR; CESO assignment work session; Stichting Vonzell – using rainforest land for social enterprise; Main port – Paramaribo; Central plaza in Paramaribo; Cannons at Fort Nieuw Amsterdam; Fort Zeelander Museum; Entrance at Plantage Friedricksdorp; Johan and Margaretha historic plantation village; Souvenirs at the Aruba Airport; Keizerstraat Mosque and Neveh Shalom Jewish Synagogue

About Jamaica

Jamaica is in the Caribbean, south of Cuba and west of Haiti. It has a population of, just under three million people. Jamaica was a British colony since 1655 and gaining its independence in 1962. It is part of the British Commonwealth today, just like Canada. Although Jamaican English is the official language, Jamaican Patois, a form of Creole, is the most widely spoken language in the country. The mainstays of the economy are tourism, agriculture, and the mining of bauxite which is used in the production of aluminum. [5] People told me that the economy has been doing well as of late, but just like everywhere else, they would like it to perform even better. In Kingston, the capital city, it was apparent there were people living in difficult circumstances. Good times for some are not always good times for all.

The CESO Assignment

I visited Jamaica in the first two weeks of December 2019. For this CESO assignment, I was asked to complete a strategic business plan for the Caribbean Climate Innovation Centre (CCIC). I worked with the CCIC staff—Carlington Burrell, Chief Administrator; Tamika Lee, Project Coordinator, and with the manager of the Science Research Council (SRC). We participated in some intensive working sessions together. After a few sessions, we updated the strategic plan, quite successfully it seemed. However, things are not always as they seem.

In going through the financial section of the plan, staff conveyed to me the core issue they wanted addressed. CCIC had been in operation since 2014. At that time, Carlington informed me that foreign aid from countries including the US, Canada (through Global Affairs Canada), and other countries had raised in $700,000 US dollars for CCIC operations. Those funds aided a lot of businesses, and they furthered climate change action initiatives. However, receiving donor funding for administration costs such as staff wages and benefits and office functions is most often not possible. Foreign donor funding is usually for projects - tangible and transparent controllable expenditures that can be accountable for. Apparently, CCIC staff had not been paid since late in

2018 which was more than a year. Resolving administrative funding and wages were at the top of their list.

I proposed a cost-sharing formula to fund the administration costs between the CARICOM members. CARICOM is an organization of fourteen states throughout the Caribbean, where there are areas of economic integration and cooperation among members. Most CARICOM countries benefited from CCIC programs. My report suggested each CARICOM member contribute a pro-rated portion of funding to support administration costs. The 2018 funding percentage amounts received by each CARICOM country were suggested as a baseline for a formula. In this way, the proportional share to be contributed by all, could be fairly applied. Jamaica and Trinidad Tobago received about 60 percent of the CARICOM funding from CCIC for that year. For the other countries, the share would not seem to be too much of a burden. CCIC staff agreed this seemed reasonable, but I sensed disappointment in the faces of CCIC staff. They were hoping for a quick fix to having their wages paid. They were hoping Canada could be a reliable lone source of ongoing future funding toward those wages and administrative costs, but I could not make that a reality. Their jobs were certainly not secure, and I sensed their disappointment. I felt bad for them.

St Jago High School Visit

As part of the assignment background, Carlington took me to Spanish Town, about a thirty-minute drive from Kingston. I could see that Carlington was a great promoter for the CCIC, and he was investigating the potential for a project at St. Jago High School. I accompanied him to school, where a priority was placed on educating the students about climate change. There were a few science teachers at the meeting, and some of the bright students were asked to give presentations on their school projects. It was an interesting morning. I think those kids will have a great future.

Emancipation Park and the Four Seasons Hotel

Clarita travelled to Jamaica and joined me for the last week of my assignment. Her flight was on time, and she made it without delays or problems. On the way back to the hotel, we visited Emancipation Park; it was beautifully landscaped and had impressive sculptures. The naked statues were very revealing and did not leave much to the imagination.

We then went back to our home base at the Four Seasons Hotel in Kingston. It was an attractive resort hotel and was also impeccably manicured. The hotel was gated, with security. I was informed that Kingston had a high crime rate, so it was a good thing there was security. Kingston, in some ways, reminded me of San Pedro Sula in Honduras, with lots of gates, walls, barbed wire, and security.

The Airport Drive to Kingston

Jamaica experiences severe hurricanes, I was told, on average every four years. Hurricane Gilbert in 1988 left its mark, causing great destruction at the Norman Manley Airport, killing thirty people, and destroying 100,000 homes in Kingston. [6]. When travelling to or from that airport, you see large breakwater rock piles along the causeway, placed there to protect the roadway, airport terminals, and runways from potential storm surges, devastating winds, and flooding. The ride from that airport to the downtown was quite unsightly. There were large cement batch-plant factories, the country's largest prison, and several industries. That scenery was not a welcoming site for visitors coming to Kingston from that airport. On our way back to the airport, there was a checkpoint on the highway near to where the prison was located. I am not sure why. Our taxi was checked briefly, but we were waved ahead. That was a good thing.

During the stay in Jamaica, Carman Gagnon, a CESO advisor from Montreal, was also working on an assignment in Kingston, and she was staying at the Four Seasons Hotel where Clarita and I were. I had run into Carman on another assignment in Bulacan State University in the Philippines, three months earlier. Carman was a great companion for us, and we did some fun things together. We had a weekend off from the work assignment, so we all travelled together from Kingston to Montego Bay, which is on the opposite side of Jamaica - it is amazingly beautiful.

We stayed at the Sea Garden Resort. It was more of an older, historic hotel, but great food at the buffet, a fantastic ocean beach, and with outstanding landscaping and natural vegetation. If anybody is looking for a delightful place to stay in Montego Bay, this is it.

Reggie Music—Entertainment at the Hotel

Jamaica is where reggae music originated, and the home of the late Bob Marley. Each night at the hotel, there was entertainment—always reggae. I did not listen to or know much about reggae music before this trip, but I must admit, I have an appreciation for it now. The singers at the hotel were really animated and after a song or two, the place was really hopping.

The Land Tour at Montego Bay

In addition to relaxing and enjoying the sights of Montego Bay, we went on a land tour of the area. Highlights of the land tour featured several interesting things. We visited a magnificent mansion, with a powerful view overlooking the bay and the city. This luxurious palace was an architectural masterpiece containing classic furniture, impressive sculptures, fancy mirrors, and expensive artwork. I do not think anybody lives there anymore, but it is now a museum, and it takes a large workforce to look after house and grounds. To contrast this luxurious palace, our tour travelled through the lower-class slum areas of Montego Bay. This contrast between Montego Bay living standards in different areas was shocking.

The next stop was at the central plaza. Many people were gathered there to buy things at the small shops and eat food. The local favourite food to be enjoyed is the famous Jamaican jerk chicken.

Statues of the Heros

Along the main street going into the downtown of Montego Bay was a small square in the front of some shops, and it was called the Circle of Heroes—there were statues of Jamaica's formidable heroes—including Bob Marley and Usain

Bolt. These gentlemen define Jamaica. Bob Marley for his famous musical accomplishments and Usain Bolt for being an Olympic world record holder in track—in the 100- and 200-meter races. That makes him the fastest sprinter in the world. Jamaica is so proud of their heroes.

The Ocean Tour and the Catamaran Boat Cruise at Montego Bay

The catamaran boat cruise took place on a warm sunny day in Jamaica. The sky was clear and blue, the ocean calm and inviting. It was the second week of December, and there were lots of younger people onboard. That was why the term "booze" cruise was used to refer to that experience. It was noisy, and alcohol was in abundance. Carman, Clarita, and I were quite mellow at first, but eventually we mingled with some of the folks—but we behaved well and did nothing to harm the reputation of Canada. The catamaran stopped at a reef and all passengers were encouraged to go snorkeling. I did, and it was nice. I could not coax those two ladies to join me. They should have because it was a lot of fun. As we went ashore, the Jamaican sunset happened. It was spectacular. It was absolutely perfect.

The Bob Marley Museum

Back in Kingston, there were more things to see. We visited the Bob Marley Museum. This man invented reggae - a unique style of Jamaican music now celebrated around the world. The museum displayed photos, information, and artifacts depicting his life. It also contained the wall plaques of his golden records and other achievements. I think Jamaica will always celebrate reggae music, in addition to its world-class Olympic track and field stars, and jerk chicken.

Blue Mountain Coffee

Jamaica claims to one of the best coffee producers in the world. Blue Mountain Coffee is a well-known brand both within and outside of Jamaica. There was a tour guide named Lincoln at the Four Seasons Hotel in Kingston, and I asked him to take me up to the high mountains where Blue Mountain Coffee is produced. I wanted to compare these operations with those I saw in Colombia. Unfortunately, it was Sunday, and upon arrival at the mountain, we learned that there were no coffee demonstrations for tourists that day. I was hoping to see the growing, picking, sorting, roasting, and grinding taking place. I did get to go on a hike, see the coffee plantation, and enjoy the views from the Blue Mountains, the highest mountains in Jamaica. Although the area was interesting, there were extra charges, and it had been my understanding that the tour was a fixed price. For the few hours in the afternoon, that tour was overpriced, as it was higher than indicated on the brochures. I was not informed that many of the site features were closed on the Sunday. I did not get my money's worth on this tour, and I was quite disappointed.

Port Royal

A part of that coffee tour included visiting the historic Fort Charles located in the town of Port Royal, near to Kingston. This was the oldest fort built in Jamaica. It was constructed between 1650 and 1660, according to the historic plaque at the wall. Because it was Sunday, the fort gates were locked, and there was no entry. I was told that the fort was in bad shape because of damage incurred from the most recent hurricane. Areas of that fort were placarded with signs forbidding entry. Other than some solid brick walls and a few historic cannons on the grounds, this was a complete waste of time. The time getting there was also added to the cost for that tour.

While driving through the Town of Port Royal, I stopped and spoke to a fisherman. I thought I might plan to go fishing for a few hours if I could find some time to do that. But, as it turned out, there was no time to fit that into the schedule while in Jamaica. There are some big fish to be caught in the Caribbean.

As we were driving near the Norman Manley Highway close to the airport, I noticed some strange landscape. I thought Jamaica was a tropical country. Just off a pathway, there was some desert vegetation including the Saguaro cactus. I thought these were found in Arizona, not Jamaica.

Ocho Rios

While I was working on the CESO assignment in Kingston, Clarita took a one-day excursion to Ocho Rios, which is a ninety-minute bus ride to the west coast of Jamaica. While there, she rode a horse along the beach, went on a zip-line, toured the area, and ate a great seafood meal. She had a wonderful time. That day, she was having an adventure just like Indiana Jones. If I had not had CESO work that day, I would have loved to have gone with her.

Traffic Congestion Beyond Belief

On my last day in Jamaica, I was working at the CCIC offices, and it was time to go back to the hotel. It was Jamaica's version of Black Friday, about three weeks before Christmas, and everyone in Kingston was out doing their Christmas shopping that day. As I was ready to leave, the CCIC office phoned for a taxi for me, but they were booked solid. It was normally a half hour ride back to the hotel from the CCIC office. It started to get dark outside, and although I was inside a fenced compound where the CCIC offices were located, I started to get scared. What if I could not get a taxi? The flight to Canada was scheduled to leave the next morning. My cell phone was dead.

As time passed, the guard at the gate continued to phone for a taxi. The online response said it would come in thirty minutes. It did not. The guard phoned again, multiple times. The promises to come and pick me up kept being made, but they were not fulfilled. Finally, after two and a half hours, a taxi came. It was my most reliable cab driver Wayne—he had other commitments, but he went out of his way to help me out.

On the last evening in Jamaica, my wife had plans for us to go out for dinner with Carman. But I got back to the hotel too late. Upon my return, I saw Clarita and Carman in the hotel restaurant. I joined them, but it was not the evening that was planned. It was our last night in Jamaica and a bit of a stressful way to end that trip.

The next morning, Wayne our most dependable taxi driver took Clarita and I to the airport. It was time to go back home to Canada.

Jamaica in The Rear View Mirror

Jamaica was interesting and an exceptionally beautiful place. It is a wonderful place to spend a relaxing vacation. However, it seemed as if everything I wanted to buy was expensive, and there was little room for negotiating the price, as is usually the case in other developing countries. I do not like to be too negative, but there was always a feeling that you were paying more for things than you should be, so be careful when shopping or spending money in Jamaica.

There is something unique and special about Jamaica, and you can easily enjoy the beauty and its fun-loving people. This is encapsulated by the Bob Marley song, "Don't worry, be happy!" That is very much the Jamaican character. Jamaicans are very good at not letting stress get to them. They just go with the flow, talk a lot, and enjoy their lives.

FOOTNOTES

1. World Population Prospect; United Nations, (November 2019); as cited in Wikipedia

2. www.foxbusiness.com, (September 21, 2016); as cited in Wikipedia

3. Overall total population – World Population Prospects; United Nations Department of Economic and Social Affairs (November 2019 revision); as cited in Wikipedia

4. Migge, Bettina; Léglise, Isabelle; Bartens, Angela, Creoles in Education: An Appraisal of Current Programs and Projects (2010); as cited in Wikipedia

5. The CIA World Factbook – Jamaica (September 16, 2015) as cited in Wikipedia

6. Gil Clark, Preliminary Report Hurricane Gilbert in 1988 (GIF) (Report). 1988 Atlantic Hurricane Season: Atlantic Storm Wallet Digital Archives, National Hurricane Center (November 26, 1988) as cited in Wikipedia

Pictures of Jamaica

From top left: A Jamaica sunset; CESO assignment SWOT analysis session 2019 – Jamaica; CCIC – Caribbean Climate Innovation Center staff; St. Jago High School students and teachers; CESO VA Carmon Gagnon, Clarita and myself in Montego Bay; With Clarita at Emancipation Park; Unattractive drive to Norman Manley Airport – Kingston; A desert in Jamaica – near Port Royal; Cannons on the outer walls of Port Royal; Jamaican landscape on a hazy day; Sea Garden Resort in Montego Bay; Nightly Entertainment at the Sea Garden Resort

Pictures of Jamaica

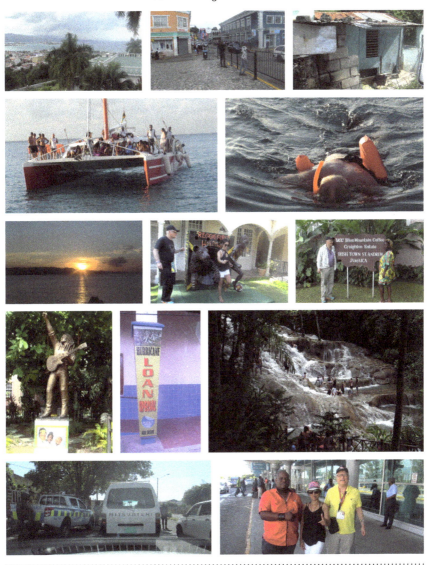

From top left: A view from a museum mansion in Montego Bay; Montego Bay city centre; Substandard housing in Montego Bay; The catamaran tour; Snorkeling in the waters of Jamaica; Another spectacular Jamaican sunset; Clarita at Circle of Heroes (Jamaican); The Blue Mountain Coffee Estate; Bob Marley Museum; Loans for hurricane damages; Ocho Rios; Checkpoint on our way to the airport; Wayne our taxi driver;
> Picture of the Bob Marley Museum and the picture of the falls at Ocho Rio are courtesy of Creative Commons Free Stock Photos

Chapter 14

....

CONCLUSION

Nearly a Decade of Volunteering for CESO
and the Adventures Travelling Abroad

Why did I author this book? It took a lot of patience and work. Memories, experiences, and unusual events from my travels abroad are etched in my brain. They are unforgettable to me, and I thought they might be worth sharing. Yes, there was a bit of everything in my travels . . . happiness and joy, excitement and fun, fear and danger, accomplishment and sometimes disappointment. The travel experience and the CESO work undertaken have made my life richer and have broadened my perspectives on life, much greater than I could have ever imagined.

I began writing this book in early 2020. The coronavirus pandemic took hold throughout the world, and it changed my world changed as it did for most people. Suddenly, I had a lot of "stay at home" time on my hands. I started to draft this book and once beginning, I could not stop. The book is very personal and precious to me. First, is my desire to share these stories with my family and my friends. I think many of you were aware I was going away on these trips, but you did not know what I was doing, or why was I going to these places. You know that now. There may be readers who may wish to read a book about far away unknown places, unique cultures and pristine environments. There may also be readers who do volunteer work for non-government agencies (NGO's) who have travelled abroad and who could identify with the work and challenges which I described. I have provided information in this book on environmental management and sustainable development themes, and this may be interesting for urban planners and environmental managers and policymakers. This book is a "mixed-bag" of observations, experiences, and adventures, and I hope they will be amusing and helpful to those who chose to readers it.

There are some striking "take aways" from these travels.

I had been told—that Canadians are well respected in the world and our country is highly regarded—mostly true. I have always been extremely proud to be a Canadian, and even more now. I do not recall any interaction where there was negativity expressed toward Canada. I have heard other Canadians who travel say this — I can attest that this is true.

Our country of Canada, by comparison with others, is well-governed, inclusive, and generous. We are truly fortunate. We have a high standard of living, a social safety net, and established rights and freedoms. Most countries do not offer citizens such a safe and comfortable framework. The troubling part is that when I return to Canada from a less fortunate country, it takes me a month or more to return to normal—physically, mentally, and emotionally. In many countries, I have seen a lot of poverty, and people living in underprivileged circumstances. While travelling, I saw desperate people begging for money or food in the street. It is troubling to see that. For me, it is frustrating when I come home and hear Canadians complain so much. Often, Canadians complain about things that are not so important. Why do we complain so much? It seems to me our society has become obsessed with self-interest, materialism, and things that are superficial and far from the core of who we are as human beings.

Canadians can learn so much from other countries that are less fortunate. I observed that most people in these poorer countries are more resilient, kind, respectful, and caring. People tend to be less self-centered and individualistic. In my now seven decades as a citizen of Canada, there seems to be a value shift taking place. It appears we are "drifting away" from those values of modesty, resilience, and compassion, which I think were imprinted in previous generations of Canadian. Events such as the depression of the 1930s and two world wars helped Canadians to embrace a higher level of character through the twentieth century and the years in which my own values and beliefs were passed down to me. I observed this in my parents, relatives, and in the older generations as I was growing up. It seems that while these values and standards are fading away in Canada, they are now much more prevalent in people living in those poorer countries which I visited. It saddens me to see that most of us who live in the Western world are losing our better qualities.

There is no better way of experiencing our world than to travel and expose yourself to unique ways of life. When you wander off the beaten path and into remote areas of foreign countries, you may find many pleasant surprises. For me, it was an authentic look at life through a lens much different than my own. A very, very precious experience . . . never to be forgotten.

Which country did I like best, or which country was better than the others during my travels? One might expect that an instant favourite would come to mind. But that is not the case. Everywhere I went, I found a new and unique experience. Every place had its own special qualities, some negative but many positive attributes. The Philippines, Colombia, Ethiopia, Honduras, Mongolia, Suriname, or Jamaica were all very beautiful and interesting places. I would visit them all again. Of course, China is now on the bottom of my list. That was a place I did not feel so comfortable, even in 2017.

Life is an adventure, even after sixty. As time goes by, opportunities may be fewer, and aging may limit the mobility once enjoyed. But there may be a few more adventures to be had. I hope so. Regardless, I have been blessed to have had a great life after sixty.

ACKNOWLEGEMENTS

I received a lot of kind assistance, support and encouragement in my journey towards completing this book. There are many who I need to thank for this. First of all, my family named Smith – in West Kelowna, and Vancouver Island - Campbell River and Gabriola in British Columbia and in Steinbach, Manitoba. Firstly, my wife Clarita and kids Nicole, Riley, Dylan and Danika accompanied me on some of the travels to the Philippines and Hong Kong and we enjoyed many experiences together. Clarita was able to accompany me while on the CESO assignment in Jamaica as well. Her family in Tarlac Philippines treated us like royalty while we were in that country and her brother June (Artemio) was a very excellent tour guide and driver. I was away from home for significant amounts of time, so thank you to my family in West Kelowna. Sacrifices were made, in order to allow me to go.

Secondly - my older children Lance and Terra. Lance, my oldest son helped me a lot. He accompanied me on my first trip to Colombia and it was wonderful to have him along. He provided a presentation on marketing as part of my assignment in Colombia and he did a skype session for my Luban assignment in the Philippines as well. In addition to this, he provided me with some advice and technical assistance on the layout of the pictures and images used for the book. His assistance was huge. Terra always wanted to know where I was and what I was up to while travelling. She was my main lifeline to Canada and her unexpected phone call, while I was taking my first step onto the Great Wall of China will forever be etched in my mind.

Thirdly, my brother Bob and my sister-in-law Maggie in Manitoba, were very supportive. Bob, in particular, helped me as a third party, doing book editing. He has always been my big brother and he gave me good advice and guidance through the process of putting this book together. He was a great coach.

The writing of this book would not have been possible without CESO – the Canadian Executive Service Organization. I have been a volunteer advisor since 2011 and the organization has afforded me the opportunity to travel abroad to many countries and now write about them. The CESO staff within Canada and the country representatives in other parts of the world, were excellent and they made sure that I was comfortable and well taken care of.

Also, Anna Muir, the Communications Director for CESO provided editing, guidance and some comments regarding the book and I am very grateful for that as well.

During the CESO assignments, the hosts in the countries visited were extremely hospitable, and the drivers and boatmen providing transportation, the hotel staff and the tour guides – they all contributed to the rich experiences described in this report and I am so thankful for the kindness extended to me.

I need to mention two other gentlemen. Mike Seibert, a professional engineer and friend helped me with two skype online sessions during the assignment on energy management at Bulacan State University in the Philippines. This assignment was very successful. Paul Dupuis, a fellow planner and friend also provided some edits for me and offered some useful comments as well.

I have been an urban planner for many years. My education, qualifications and experience achieved in areas such as economic development, environmental management, strategic planning and project management were useful credentials for many international assignments. These served me well in my work with CESO. Thank you to the University of Manitoba and the Canadian Institute of Planners / Planning Institute of BC and to the many communities where I have worked – these helped me to become comfortable and competent in the role as a volunteer advisor.

Dr. Carlos Teixiera is a professor of Geography at the University of British Columbia, Okanagan also deserves a thank you. Every year since 2007, I present a guest lecture for his classes and the lectures are usually based on international CESO assignments which were undertaken. Carlos told me on several occasions, that I should write a book encapsulating my international assignment experiences. Well Carlos, I have taken your advice.

My medical doctor, Dr. Marcel Lavancy grew up in Chile, South America.

He was required to give me a medical clearance prior to travel. Not only did he look after my health requirements, but he also gave me information and advice on life in Latin America. This was very helpful for me before my assignment in Colombia.

Finally, I want to thank Friesen Press for all their help and assistance. It was Marc Brick who got me excited about writing this book and engaging Friesen Press. It was Jess Feser who managed my file and putting all the elements of this book together. Without their expertise and encouragement, this project would not have happened.

Thank you all. You help made this overwhelming project much easier than it would have been.